THE PROVEN FRAMEWORK THAT
TURNS YOUR VISION INTO REALITY

AN OPERATIONAL FRAMEWORK

EMMA RAINVILLE

FOREWORD BY: PERRY BELCHER
CONTRIBUTORS: RICHARD PARKIN & TRAVIS GOMEZ

Library of Congress Control Number: 2024921890

eBook ISBN: 978-1-965092-82-8
Paperback ISBN: 978-1-965092-80-4
Hardcover ISBN: 978-1-965092-81-1

1. Main category—Business & Money › Business Development & Entrepreneurship › Entrepreneurship
2. Other category—Self-Help › Time Management
3. Other category—Business & Money › Management & Leadership › Production & Operations

First Edition

Published by: AR PRESS
Roger L. Brooks, Publisher
roger@americanrealpublishing.com
americanrealpublishing.com

Table of Contents

This book is dedicated to my business partner Travis Gomez. Thank you for always believing in me. Thank you for choosing me, pushing me, tolerating me, teaching me, fighting with me… thank you for all of it. I love you more than you'll ever know.

Thank you to my team at Shockwave. You guys make me look like a rock star every day, and I appreciate you all so much.

Richard Parkin, you are such an incredible human being. I love taking this journey with you. Thank you for telling me when I'm wrong and standing beside me anyway. You are the greatest hire of my career, and I'm grateful to now call you partner.

Ryan Pottet: everyone should have a "Ryan." Thank you for being mine.

Perry Belcher, words cannot express how thankful I am to you. You've taught me more than any other human being I've ever known. I forgot what life was like before you, and I don't want to ever experience it without you so you have to die first.

Foreword by Perry Belcher

Emma Rainville is an acquired taste.

A little bit goes a long way, like a strong medicine.

...and like medicine, it may not always be pleasant, but the objective is to get well, right?

The day I met Emma, I was in pain.

You could say I was sick, or at least that my business was.

Everything was disorganized; I didn't have standard operating procedures, financial controls, or even accurate reporting.

Contracts with vendors, joint venture partners, and employees were functionally non-existent.

Everything ran on a handshake and a good word.

Even worse, our quality control was disastrous.

In short, I was selling myself into a brick wall at 1000 miles an hour.

Not only was I sick, but I was terminal; I just didn't know it yet.

Those are the days that I refer to as B.E. or Before Emma.

I was at an industry event with a lot of people that I respect, and I saw Emma speak on stage.

She seemed to be kind of a reluctant speaker who certainly didn't have a warm and fuzzy vibe, but I noticed how many people I respected kept giving her credit for their success.

I was trying to figure out exactly what she did.

Was she some sort of marketing guru?

Was she a traffic expert?

Was she some great genius product developer?

The truth is, Emma is none of those things.

She's kind of like those old BASF commercials: she just makes all those things better.

I remember going over and introducing myself to her and asking if we could get on a phone call to talk about my business so that I could soothe my curiosity.

Frankly, she seemed like she could care less but agreed.

When we hopped on the call and I laid out my problems, Emma lit up.

I've never seen anybody quite like her. She loves a problem like a fat kid loves cake; it's a puzzle to her.

We made an arrangement, I went through the SCOPE process and I hired Emma and her team to come in and be my fractional COO, handling all forms of operation in my business.

As soon as everyone knew that Emma was working with me, I started getting emails from people telling me to watch out because Emma rubs people the wrong way sometimes.

To tell you the truth, they were absolutely right.

Emma does not suffer fools.

She is straightforward and expects excellence in delivery from anyone, be it an employee, a vendor, a partner, etc.

She's really good to have on your side.

Fast forward two years, or A.E., and my businesses couldn't even be recognized as the same as before.

I have contracts and agreements in place, lock-solid terms of service, crystal clear books and records, and SOPs in every aspect of the business so that I don't have to depend on any one person should something go awry.

Most importantly of all, I have a friend.

One who is objectively critical, a foil of sorts, who tells me when I'm about to screw up but will still let me do it just to teach me a lesson sometimes.

Emma is not a good marketer, but she knows good marketing from bad.

She's a terrible salesperson, especially when it comes to selling herself and her abilities.

She has a lousy bedside manner but is "let me go get the shovel" loyal.

My entire business career has changed because of Emma Rainville, and if you read what's in her book, maybe yours will too.

The truth is, most business owners are too soft to take the hard lines Emma takes. But if you can, it will change your business, and if you can't, you need to find yourself an Emma.

But you can't have mine.

Good luck, and congratulations on the book, Emma; it's fantastic.

Perry Belcher, co-founder of Digital Marketer, GrowthHacking.com, Conventions.com, and a whole bunch of other crap on the interwebs.

INTRODUCTION

I have had enormous success creating millions in profits for company after company. A major part of that success comes from having read some of the greatest business books of all time, books that have changed the landscape for thousands of businesses. I wanted to take all that I learned, along with the key components and philosophies I used to create proven success, and put it all in one place.

The thing about reading books is that you are often panning for nuggets. There's so much to get through before you *finally* come across the point they were trying to make. You can spend hours and hours reading about how great the authors are, their accomplishments, etc.

Sure, some of that might be necessary to sell the book, but it won't do a thing for your business.

While it goes against every piece of advice I've been given about marketing this book, I am going to speak briefly about myself and my company. The way I look at it is that you already have the book in your hand. You don't need to be sold.

I've built a business called Shockwave Solutions that helps business owners create vision, structure, and scalability; increase profits; and successfully implement exit strategies. It's not because I have a brilliant mind or because I took a million business courses.

It's because I was able to seek out other successful business owners, read a ton of books (head to readscope.co/thanks for the reading list I used to write this book), and mimic the things that move the needle for my clients. By doing this, I have achieved success over and over again.

In this book, I will help you get a detailed look at where you are with your business with an unfiltered eye, and how to create the path you *actually* want to be on.

By reading this *one* book, you can learn from what I was able to construct after reading hundreds of them, implementing and testing those theories in dozens of businesses, and creating an operational framework with proven success.

In this book, you will learn:

❖ How to eradicate every business-related frustration you are currently facing.

❖ How to elevate your staff with leadership and mentorship while giving them a vision and a path to success.

❖ How to lead meetings that stay on track, are useful to your business, and that drive your vision forward every time.

❖ How to make sure all your employees at every level understand your vision, learn how to be battle buddies instead of co-workers, and start to establish real accountability.

❖ How to stay on target and not get distracted by shiny objects.

❖ How to keep control over your time and deliver on your goals.

❖ How to focus on increasing profits rather than revenue alone.

❖ How to avoid stagnation and push constantly forward past any obstacles.

❖ How to build your organization for the long haul and not be seduced by the dangerous "quick fixes" that leave many companies worse off.

❖ How to use our library of skills, tools, and systems to optimize your staff and process execution, leadership, and company-wide communications to achieve your vision.

❖ How to decrease stress levels and take better care of yourself so that you can be the powerful leader your organization and vision require you to be.

Within this book, you'll find all the tools to create a framework of operations that no one in your team will question, everybody understands, and everyone is committed to maintaining.

In every how-to business book you've read, the authors have likely branded their own operating system to codify their methodology. But here's the thing: when it comes to an operating system for an organization, it can *never* be one-size-fits-all.

Your processes need to be custom-fitted to you and your organization's specific needs to achieve the best outcomes in the most appropriate timeframe. In this book, you will learn the most powerful and effective way to create that custom-fit operational system.

Few things will be more valuable to your organization than an operational framework; it will let you recruit your staff based on your company's values, provide a shared language and framework for your team, and serve as your company's bulletin for decision-making. When you see one team member citing from your custom operating system as they support another team member, you'll likely swell with pride and confidence in your business's ability to succeed and fulfill your dreams. And that, after all, is what it's all about.

At Shockwave Solutions, the company Travis Gomez and I have built together, our foundational framework—the foundation our company is built on—is called *WAVE.*

Foundational Frameworks are not the same as *operational* frameworks, which your company uses to maintain and sustain itself. I will dive more into both later.

In this book, I'll show you how to build your own foundational framework, WAVE, and your operational framework, SCOPE.

What Is SCOPE?

I developed SCOPE with my team some time ago. Each letter stands for something of high operational importance that contributes to the creation of your operating system.

S - Setting your Vision
C - Create Processes
O - Operational Excellence
P - People Development
E - Execution ——----> Move

SCOPE will give you a step-by-step view of your company and how to move the needle on your overall operations.

We will begin with S—Setting your Vision—for a reason.

You first need to put your story, your vision on paper, to craft an inspiring one-page document that lays out your vision for growth, clearly defines your team's values, and highlights your company's journey from past to present and into a promising future—a tangible document that everyone in your organization can look at every day.

This powerful tool will not only guide your daily operations but also reignite your passion and hope for what lies ahead. Without it, you'll never be able to keep your team on the same page.

That's just step one. By the end, you're going to achieve a state of operational excellence for your business, where everything operates smoothly and effectively. You get to work *on* your business, not just *in* it.

Most entrepreneurs worry about a thousand different things. We will outline all the key components of putting together a customized operating system for your organization to get you to hyperfocus on just a few. Those few key components will keep your organization's health in great shape.

Take Chick-fil-A, for example. No matter how you feel about them as a company, I think everyone can agree that they always have a long line, but they still have really short wait times. Anyone who has been to Chick-fil-A will tell you they had a great experience, and not because they are hyperfocused on the spotless kitchen, the best-in-the-industry food quality, the clean bathrooms, the stocked condiment displays, or the sparkling dining room.

They hyperfocus on one thing: customer experience. Every customer who walks through the door at Chick-fil-A *must* have the best fast food experience they've ever had—nothing more, nothing less. So every team member works to ensure that every customer has the best customer experience they've ever had at any fast food restaurant. *Because* of that, the kitchens are spotless, the food is of high quality, the bathrooms are kept clean, the condiments are always well-stocked, the dining rooms are sparkling clean, and on and on and on.

See? YOU DON'T HAVE TO NITPICK A MILLION TINY THINGS to ensure everything is functioning properly and efficiently. What matters is finding the one thing that underpins them—that smaller, clearer hyperfocus.

So how do you do that? How do you find that one thing?

The first step is identifying some very important components of your custom operating system. Once we do that, you can put together your ONE THING!

Part 1
Setting Your Vision:

WAVE

What is WAVE? It is the structure you'll use to make that one-page roadmap to your vision!

Your company's WAVE can be created in two days of focused, uninterrupted time. In this section, I'll walk you through how I create them with my visionaries[1].

This is the outline you will follow so you can print your story on an easy-to-read, one-page poster that all the members of your organization can refer to for direction, focus, and inspiration.

Step 1: Written Vision

Putting your vision down on paper seems like it would be super easy, right? Well, for some, it's one of the most difficult things they will ever do. Being honest with yourself and your capabilities and

---

1   Visionaries are individuals who possess a clear, forward-thinking vision for the future of a business or project. They are often characterized by their ability to see opportunities where others may not, setting long-term goals and inspiring others with their innovative ideas. Visionaries typically focus on big-picture strategies and the overall direction of an organization, leaving the detailed execution to others.

aligning what you want in your professional life with what you want in your personal life can be challenging.

But that's not where the challenge ends. Visionary entrepreneurs assume that everyone on their team already knows exactly what's expected of them. As an agency-model COO and operations team, we see that time and time again.

When Shockwave takes on new clients, we run an assessment as a first step, and one of the first questions we ask is about the company's vision. When we talk to the owners and entrepreneurs, they tell us over and over that everyone understands and is committed to the company's vision.

But the second we talk to the team themselves, we see a very different picture. Never once—literally never once, has our team assessed an organization and found that claim to be true.

Generally, everyone has some idea of the vision or the future, but never has *everyone* in the organization aligned with what the owner told us.

This is why we start with a two-day offsite. We take our client's major decision-makers, usually the executive team, and put them in a large Airbnb, a hotel with a conference room, or a similar location for some uninterrupted time.

I prefer the weekends, when it's easier to get everyone's mind away from the day-to-day business and into what makes the business work. During that time, we create their organization's one-page poster ... WAVE.

Shockwave is named after what an earthquake causes: shock-waves. All the terms we use within our organization relate to that. I call this poster a WAVE, but you can call it whatever makes sense for you.

We have repeatedly seen an organizational shift in our clients within weeks of launching their written vision. Morale increases dramatically, co-workers begin to work as battle buddies instead of strangers who work together, and the company starts completing tasks and crushing goals.

Like SCOPE, WAVE is an acronym,

W - Written Vision
A - Absolute Focus
V - Values Driven Future
E - Execution Plan

Let's dive in on the "W" in WAVE. This is your **Written Vision.**

It consists of four planned-out sections.

First, your 10-Year Glimpse statement—a simple paragraph that describes what things look like in your business ten years from now.

Your 5- and 3-Year Flash Forwards are more thought-out. Each one contains five to ten milestones for your organization, along with approximate revenue and profits.

Finally, we will drill into your 1-Year Commitments. Depending on the size of your organization, this is a list of five to fifteen things you *will* accomplish this year to drive your business closer to your 10-Year Glimpse statement.

While that process sounds pretty simple, it takes a lot of time and specific considerations. This piece will get everyone in your organization rowing in the same direction. It's going to be game-changing …

Are you ready to create your WAVE? At the end of this section, you'll see some templates for each exercise. You can download a copy from readscope.co/tools.

Let's get started with the 10-Year Glimpse statement. The point of this exercise is to map out where you will be ten years from today and to ensure that this is realistic, without any contradictions between your personal and professional goals.

Imagine that the ghost of Christmas Future arrived at your bedside and took you forward ten years.

When we start this exercise, spend some time thinking through what your personal life looks like today. Now think of how you want it to look in ten years.

Do you have a spouse? If you have children, how old are they today? Now imagine them ten years older. Will you have more children? How old will they be in ten years?

Now, imagine your interactions with your spouse and children. How involved are you? Are you having dinner with them every night? Are you walking your children to school each morning? Do you go to their baseball, soccer, or basketball games? Do you watch their gymnastics competitions?

Are you a scout leader? Do you attend church or any civic meetings regularly? Where do you live? How many hours a week do you skip your personal life to work on or in your business?

Now the ghost of Christmas Future brings you to your office. You arrive at your office window and get a high-level overview of your business operations.

What does it look like? How many employees do you have?

What products are you selling, or what services are you providing? What is your customer avatar? What is your demographic?

What is the annual revenue, and how does it differ from today? What are the primary roles of your employees? What does your executive team consist of?

Describe on paper what you see. Do you have an open floor plan office? Is everyone working remotely? Are you working from a lake house?

Put pen to paper and describe everything. Are you still in the same position, or have you replaced yourself?

Once you have done the exercises, read through *both* of them. *Do they align?*

Have you built an empire that you are running, but you get home for dinner every night and ride bikes with your kids to school every morning?

Those things do not align. I am sorry, but they just do not.

We have found that visionary entrepreneurs tend to live in a *parallel universe* to the rest of us. They dream big, aim higher, and can usually achieve more in a reasonable timeline.

They cannot conceptualize how long tasks and projects will take when they run concurrently with other projects and the daily tasks that come with running a business. Coupled with the shiny new objects they like to throw at their staff, this often leads to frustration and the feeling that "no one can keep up with me."

With the right formula, visionaries can aspire to reach the stars, but it's important to have goals and not just constantly move toward shiny objects. Movement is good, but movement with purpose is greatness.

In this section, you will review what you have written for your personal and professional life and ensure that it is realistic and achievable.

Your business aspirations must accommodate the space you wish to create for your personal and family life, and it is important to hold yourself to the integrity you would want from your staff.

Are both lives possible for one person in the same lifetime?

Once you have made concessions to one or both, it's time to create your 10-Year Glimpse statement. Go through everything you wrote for your personal and professional life and eliminate, elaborate, and adjust things to align them.

Looking at all the things that are left, create three-to-five sentences about what your 10-Year Glimpse is. See the examples below from some of the visionaries I've worked with:

- ❖ Minority owner position in 100 companies

- ❖ CEO hired as owner replacement

- ❖ Board of Advisors established

- ❖ A Dozen or More Info Products, Educational Learning and Teaching, Which Shape and Impact Communities, Families, and Business Through Leadership Development

- ❖ Directly Impacting Over 1 Million Lives

- ❖ COO Services Launched

- ❖ Team Building Program Built

- ❖ COO Group Coaching Started

- ❖ 300 Full Time Customer Service Agents

It is time to move on to your 5 & 3-Year Flash Forward. This is a little more dialed in than your 10-Year Glimpse, so try to be more intentional about documenting where you want to go.

I struggled for a long time when creating this to decide whether three or five years was the mark. After much team debate and several clients who did one, the other, or both, I determined that we *needed* both. There is simply too much time between three and ten years, and far too much time from one year to five.

We intend to write down the milestones we will achieve in the next three and five years to empower our staff to make good decisions for our organization. If they do not fully understand where we are trying to go and how they are trying to get there, then they're moving without a map.

When that's the case, everyone in the organization loses out on the "why" when making decisions, which prevents them from aligning with your overall goals. Aligning everyone on where our path is heading sets the direction for key staff to lead their teams.

Just as you did with year ten, think about five years from now. To get to your 10-Year Glimpse, what must you accomplish within five years?

Re-ask yourself all those questions from the 10-Year Glimpse:

Do you have a spouse? Children? Will you have more? Imagine all of them five years older.

Imagine your family interactions. How involved are you? Dinner? School? Sports? Scouts? Are you active in your community? Where do you live? How many hours a week do you skip your personal life to work in your business?

Once again, the ghost of Christmas Future brings you to your office window to see your business operations five years from now.

What does it look like? How many employees do you have? What are your products or services, your customer avatar, and your demographic? What is the annual revenue? How many employees do you have, and what are their primary roles? What does your executive team consist of?

With the presence of mind we taught you earlier, look at your personal life and how you correlate it with how you would like to grow your business in your 5-year Flash Forward. This doesn't need to be exact, and it will not be completely accurate. Unlike your 1-Year Commitments, which we will be doing last, Flash Forwards can change and adapt with time. You can pivot when necessary.

The whole point is to have a target. It's handing your team a map to where they want to go. You can pave new roads along the way, if needed.

Now sit down and extract five to ten realistic and achievable milestones you want your team to reach in the next five years. Add in what you want your revenue and profits to be and how many employees you plan to have.

You can write in which key people you will be adding, perhaps in your C-Suite. Or maybe you want to bring paid media in-house, or perhaps customer service. Whatever you see in the story you wrote for yourself, pull out bullet points until you can clearly state what your people need to know.

Then repeat this for year three.

Now that you have laid out a map of where you want to go, it's time to get dialed in.

You will now create your 1-Year Commitments—the goals you commit to completing in the next year, no matter what. You will NOT change them, adjust them, or add to them. You are making these commitments to get one year closer to your 10-Year Glimpse Statement.

This isn't just a high-level overview of your life and business; you will get specific when imagining your future a year from now.

Start by asking yourself the following questions, and go deep:

❖ What products do you sell?

❖ How many people work for you, and what are their specific roles?

❖ What has been brought in-house, and what are you utilizing vendors for?

❖ How are you acquiring your customers?

- ❖ What revenue do you need to support your business AND the growth you are trying to accomplish?

- ❖ What is the profit margin that makes it worth it all?

- ❖ How much profit are you taking, and how much are you investing back into the business for growth?

- ❖ Visualize your interactions with your staff.

Once you've visualized your one-year picture, it's time to write out the key measurables. These should be realistic and attainable. For most businesses, the following are a must:

- ❖ What is your revenue amount specifically?

- ❖ What is your profit amount specifically?

- ❖ How many products do you sell, or how many services do you offer?

- ❖ How many employees do you have? Who is the leadership team? Have you hired a key member in this time frame?

Emma Rant:

I want to pause to talk about these questions. You should know exactly where you are right now for each of these points.

If you, as the business owner, cannot answer these questions in five minutes or less, you've failed. If you are the CEO and do not know the answers or how to look them up instantly, you've failed.

Every executive should know these Key Performance Indicators (KPIs). If EVERYONE in your C-Suite cannot do that, you've failed.

If you do not have proper books (that's true, by the way, for about 80 percent of new Shockwave clients), then you've failed. Getting them in order needs to be your Number One goal in your year one exercise. I cannot stress this enough.

If you are hell-bent on hiding your books from your C-Suite, you will never have a business that deserves a proper one. Plain and simple. If you don't want the people who are responsible for your P&L results to have access to drill into that information, then you are limiting their capability to help you.

Beyond those measurables, what are five to ten things that would mean you're on your way to accomplishing your vision? For example:

What (as close as possible) is each product or service you provide? How many marketing people do you employ? What is your cost to acquire a customer, and what are your primary traffic sources?

What departments in your organization are built out? What vendors are you primarily utilizing? Who is in your core team?

Keep looking back at your Flash Forwards and make sure you are thinking about one year from now and what you need to accomplish to achieve what's there.

Next, fill in five to fifteen goals you want to accomplish this year. These will be your commitments. You and your team will have *no* excuses for not completing these, so they must be clear and realistically accomplishable.

This isn't about setting vague, aspirational goals. It's not about what you want your team to work on. It's about tangible, clear, important steps you will take in the next year. When you set a commitment, it should be as good as done … NO EXCUSES.

Once you have established those five to fifteen commitments, it's time to think about ONE person who will be held accountable for each one.

While most big needle movers require multiple contributors, only one person can own the task. That person has to report progress to the team and work to ensure that all the pieces keep moving forward until the goal is accomplished. You're making them responsible for completing the commitment and handing them the power to do that.

Add a timeline for the commitment to make it clearer and more realistic. When does it need to be completed? When *can* it be completed?

Depending on the size of the commitment, now's the time to think about key milestones. What individual tasks need to be completed for the overall project to be completed? Add these for each of your commitments.

Finally, is your team ready to tackle each of these commitments right now, or do they need some support to get there? Write out any resources required for each of these commitments.

Step 1: Envision your future self 10 years from now.

Step 2: Consider your personal life 10 years in the future. Write answers for the following questions, and any others that matter to you:

- Are you married?
- Do you have children? How old are they?
- If you already have children, how old will they be 10 years from now? Have you had any more children?
- How involved are you with your partner and children?

  - Do you sit down to dinner with them nightly?
  - Do you take them to school in the morning?
  - Are you attending their baseball games? Other sports events?
  - Do you regularly attend church? Civic meetings?

- Where do you live?
- What does your work-life balance look like? How many hours a week do you take off of your personal life to work in or on your business?

Step 3: After exploring the personal, consider your work. Imagine that you're looking through the window of your office. Again, write answers to the following questions, and any other relevant points:

- What does the office look like?
- How many employees do you have?
- What products/ services do you sell?

- What is your customer avatar?
- Who is your demographic?
- What is your annual revenue, and how has this changed over the last 10 years?
- Who is in your executive team?
- What are the primary roles of your employees?
- Are you still in the same position, or have you replaced yourself?

Step 4: Compare your answers for both work and your personal life. Are both visions possible at the same time, or are there any contradictions between the two? Do they align?

Step 5: Whenever required, decide where you will make concessions on your vision for the future. Remove any points you've decided to take out of your future visions.

Step 6: Once you've created a more realistic, achievable vision, summarize it in 3-5 sentences. This is your 10-Year Glimpse Statement.

Step 7: Proceed to the 5 & 3-Year Flash Forward worksheet.

Note: You'll be repeating most of the steps below for both 5-year and 3-year visions of your company's future. You may find it helpful to take a break between each session, in order to reset your vision of the future.

Step 1: Envision your future self 5 years from now. Here, you should be a lot more dialed in, a lot more detailed than you were in your 10-Year Glimpse.

Step 2: What do you need to have accomplished by the 5 year mark in order to be on track to achieve your 10-Year Glimpse?

Step 3: Write answers for the following questions about your personal life, as well as any others that matter to you:

- Are you married?
- Do you have children? How old are they?
- If you already have children, how old will they be 5 years from now? Have you had any more children?
- How involved are you with your partner and children?

    ○ Do you sit down to dinner with them nightly?
    ○ Do you take them to school in the morning?
    ○ Are you attending their baseball games? Other sports events?
    ○ Do you regularly attend church? Civic meetings?

- Where do you live?
- What does your work-life balance look like? How many hours a week do you take off of your personal life to work in or on your business?

Step 4: After exploring the personal, think about your work life. Imagine that you're looking through the window of your office. Again, write answers to the following questions, and any other relevant points:

- What does the office look like?
- How many employees do you have?
- What products/ services do you sell?
- What is your customer avatar?
- Who is your demographic?
- What is your annual revenue, and how has this changed over the last 5 years?
- Who is in your executive team?
- What are the primary roles of your employees?
- Are you still in the same position, or have you replaced yourself?

Step 5: While the process of writing your 10-Year Glimpse Statement will have given you a more realistic view of your vision, take the time to compare your two answers, looking for any contradictions between the two.

Step 6: Again, make any necessary concessions.

Step 7: From this point, plan out 5-10 milestones that you will *need* to accomplish by the 5-year mark in order to achieve the reality of your 10-Year Glimpse Statement.

Step 8: What will your revenue be 5 years from now? How much of that will you retain as profit?

Step 9: How many employees will you have 5 years from now?

Step 10: Once you've created a full list of milestones, as well as the financial and employee targets, look back through the list. While Flash Forwards can be adjusted over time, the milestones should still be realistic and achievable. Make sure that everything is aligned and realistic.

Step 11: Envision your future self 3 years from now. Here, you should be a lot more dialed in than you were in your 10-Year Glimpse, and more realistic than in your 5-Year Flash Forward.

Step 12: What do you need to have accomplished by the 3 year mark in order to be on track to achieve your 10-Year Glimpse and 5-Year Flash Forward?

Step 13: Write answers for the following questions, and any others that matter to you:

- Are you married?
- Do you have children? How old are they?
- If you already have children, how old will they be 3 years from now? Have you had any more children?
- How involved are you with your partner and children?

  - Do you sit down to dinner with them nightly?
  - Do you take them to school in the morning?
  - Are you attending their baseball games? Other sports events?
  - Do you regularly attend church? Civic meetings?

- Where do you live?

- What does your work-life balance look like? How many hours a week do you take off of your personal life to work in or on your business?

Step 14: After exploring the personal, consider your work. Imagine that you're looking through the window of your office. Again, write answers to the following questions, and any other relevant points:

- What does the office look like?

- How many employees do you have?

- What products/ services do you sell?

- What is your customer avatar?

- Who is your demographic?

- What is your annual revenue, and how has this changed over the last 3 years?

- Who is in your executive team?

- What are the primary roles of your employees?

- Are you still in the same position, or have you replaced yourself?

Step 15: Again, take the time to compare your two answers, looking for any contradictions between the two, and making any necessary concessions.

Step 16: From this point, plan out 5-10 milestones that you will *need* to accomplish by the 3-year mark in order to achieve the reality of both your 10-Year Glimpse Statement and 5-Year Flash Forward.

Step 17: What will your revenue be 3 years from now? How much of that will you retain as profit?

Step 18: How many employees will you have 3 years from now?

Step 19: Once you've created a full list of milestones, as well as the financial and employee targets, look back through the list and ensure that everything is reasonable and achievable.

Step 20: Review both your 5-Year and 3-Year Flash Forwards now that they're complete. These should be in alignment, and give you a clear look at what needs to be done to meet your 10-Year Glimpse.

Step 21: With both Flash Forwards complete, move onto the 1-Year Commitments worksheet.

Step 1: At this point, consider your business a year from now. While the previous sheets have contained speculation and high-level overviews, this should be completely realistic.

Step 2: Ask yourself some specific questions about your company a year from now:

- What products/services are you selling? Are you selling any new ones?
- How many people work for you, and in what roles?
- What departments and tasks are being done in-house, and what are you utilizing vendors for?
- How are you acquiring customers? Has this changed in any way?
- What level of revenue does your business need to survive?
- What level of revenue does your business need to meet your goals?
- What profit margin are you achieving?
- How are you distributing that profit between yourself and the business?
- How do you interact with your staff?

Step 3: Start to consider KPIs and quantifiable metrics. Ask the following questions as a start:

- How much revenue are you bringing in?
- How much profit are you making?
- How many products/ services do you offer?
- How many employees do you have?

- Who is the leadership team?
- Have you made any key hires in the last year?

Step 4: Write down 5-10 things that you need to have accomplished in order to bring you and your company closer towards your 10-Year Glimpse and Flash Forwards.

Step 5: With all of the above in mind, start to write down 5-15 major goals which you want to achieve in the next year. These shouldn't be one-off, simple tasks, but accomplishments that require a significant amount of work.

Step 6: Are all of these realistically achievable within the next 12 months? If not, you will need to make some compromises.

Step 7: Decide on a finalized list of commitments which you *will* achieve in the next year.

Step 8: Assign a single team member to be responsible for each of the commitments. While many commitments will require the contribution of several team members, a single person should be accountable for the completion of the project.

Step 9: Think through the timeline for each commitment. Not all of these can or should be done at once, nor can they be left until the end of the year. When must each commitment be completed by?

Step 10: Depending on the size of each commitment, you may need to break them down into smaller tasks. Create milestones for each of your commitments that needs them.

Step 11: Think through the resources that your team will need to accomplish each commitment that they are assigned. Add these to each commitment.

Step 12: Can your team realistically accomplish each of these commitments within the year? If not, what's preventing them, and what needs to change for all your commitments to be accomplished?

Step 13: With your commitments set, move on to the Quarterly Goals worksheet.

Step 1: Envision your future self 10 years from now.

Step 2: Consider your personal life 10 years in the future. Write answers for the following questions, and any others that matter to you:

- Are you married?
- Do you have children? How old are they?
- If you already have children, how old will they be 10 years from now? Have you had any more children?
- How involved are you with your partner and children?

  - Do you sit down to dinner with them nightly?
  - Do you take them to school in the morning?
  - Are you attending their baseball games? Other sports events?
  - Do you regularly attend church? Civic meetings?

- Where do you live?
- What does your work-life balance look like? How many hours a week do you take off of your personal life to work in or on your business?

Step 3: After exploring the personal, consider your work. Imagine that you're looking through the window of your office. Again, write answers to the following questions, and any other relevant points:

- What does the office look like?
- How many employees do you have?
- What products/ services do you sell?
- What is your customer avatar?

- Who is your demographic?
- What is your annual revenue, and how has this changed over the last 10 years?
- Who is in your executive team?
- What are the primary roles of your employees?
- Are you still in the same position, or have you replaced yourself?

Step 4: Compare your answers for both work and your personal life. Are both visions possible at the same time, or are there any contradictions between the two? Do they align?

Step 5: Whenever required, decide where you will make concessions on your vision for the future. Remove any points you've decided to take out of your future visions.

Step 6: Once you've created a more realistic, achievable vision, summarize it in 3-5 sentences. This is your 10-Year Glimpse Statement.

Step 7: Proceed to the 5 & 3-Year Flash Forward worksheet.

10-Year Glimpse Statement

SHOCK*wave*

10-Year Glimpse Statement

_____
_____
_____
_____
_____
_____
_____
_____
_____
_____
_____
_____
_____
_____
_____
_____
_____
_____
_____
_____
_____
_____
_____
_____
_____
_____
_____
_____
_____
_____
_____
_____
_____
_____

SHOCK*wave*

5-Year Flash Forward

Completion Date:

Approx. Revenue: Approx. Profit:

Milestones

_____

_____

_____

_____

_____

_____

_____

_____

_____

_____

_____

_____

_____

_____

_____

_____

_____

_____

_____

_____

_____

_____

_____

_____

_____

_____

_____

_____

_____

_____

_____

_____

SHOCKwave
IMPACT PROFITS

WAVE Outline for _____   Starting Year: 20__

3-Year Flash Forward

Completion Date:

Approx. Revenue: Approx. Profit:

Milestones

_____
_____
_____
_____
_____
_____
_____
_____
_____
_____
_____
_____
_____
_____
_____
_____
_____
_____
_____
_____
_____
_____
_____
_____
_____
_____
_____
_____
_____

SHOCKwave

1-Year Commitments

Commitments

_____
_____
_____
_____
_____
_____
_____
_____
_____
_____
_____
_____
_____
_____
_____
_____
_____
_____
_____
_____
_____
_____
_____
_____
_____
_____
_____
_____
_____
_____

SHOCKwave

Absolute Focus

_____
_____
_____
_____
_____
_____
_____
_____
_____
_____
_____
_____
_____
_____
_____
_____
_____
_____
_____
_____
_____
_____
_____
_____
_____
_____
_____
_____
_____
_____
_____
_____
_____
_____

SHOCKwave

Values

_____
_____
_____
_____
_____
_____
_____
_____
_____
_____
_____
_____
_____
_____
_____
_____
_____
_____
_____
_____
_____
_____
_____
_____
_____
_____
_____
_____

SHOCKwave

Step 1: As a starting point, find the WAVE templates provided in SCOPE. This will give you a basic layout to build from, with enough space to draft out your WAVE.

Step 2: Write out your 10-Year Glimpse Statement in the relevant page. This will be one of the most immediately visible sections on your finished WAVE, ensuring that your 10-Year Glimpse is visible whenever anyone looks at WAVE.

Step 3: Add your 5-Year Flash Forward to the relevant page, including all information about your revenue and profit. As the first of the two Flash Forwards, this allows you to directly compare milestones with the points in your 10-Year Glimpse - will you be half way towards achieving your vision?

Step 4: Similarly, add your 3-Year Flash Forward to the relevant page.

Step 5: On the appropriate page, write out your 1-Year Commitments.

Step 6: Write out your Absolute Focus, using the guidance from Step 2 of the WAVE Process.

Step 7: Using the guidance from Step 3 of the WAVE Process, write out your company's Values.

Step 8: Review your WAVE in full. Are there any points that don't make complete sense in the full context of WAVE? Finalize your ideas for WAVE before having a designer turn this template into a customized, one-page poster making your company's vision absolutely clear.

Now that we have your next ten years outlined, it's time to move on to the next part of WAVE—the "A", which stands for Absolute Focus.

Step 2: Absolute Focus

One of the hardest jobs of an integrator[2] or operator is managing visionary leaders and their priorities. In most cases, the integrator *must* be good at keeping the visionary on track and preventing them from letting shiny objects derail the team.

Visionaries are constantly thinking about the newest, greatest, and most exciting things they can do. From their perspective, there is a continual series of opportunities, and failing to take advantage of them means leaving money on the table.

Far too often, though, they end up adding more and more projects to a team of people who have no idea what their true priorities are, because *everything* is presented as a priority.

We've seen the results of this time and time again: a ton of half-implemented ideas that cause fires at every turn. Frustrated team members can't get anything over the finish line, because they can't get the resources they need and don't know who to ask. We've seen companies lose thousands of dollars a month on multiple expensive services that are all doing the same thing—or doing nothing at all.

For every visionary, establishing a clear, defined focus is imperative for success. Nothing that doesn't align with that Absolute Focus should *ever* be allowed to intrude into operations.

---

2   An Integrator is a key role within an organization responsible for translating a Visionary's ideas into actionable plans and ensuring those plans are executed effectively. Integrators manage the day-to-day operations, align teams with the vision, and solve problems as they arise, ensuring that the business runs smoothly. They are often the glue that holds the organization together, bridging the gap between high-level strategy and operational efficiency.

This is the ONE THING your company should focus on, the fundamental motivation for all your existence.

Here's something I regularly tell my visionaries:

That sounds like a fantastic idea, but it doesn't align with our Absolute Focus, so you have two choices:

1) Go start another business that focuses on that idea, using other resources.

or

2) Let go of the idea.

Once Visionary and Integrator are crystal clear on the Absolute Focus and agree that everything our company does, every product it offers or service it provides, every action we take, every client we take on, etc., *must* align with that absolute focus, it's all gravy from there.

With an Absolute Focus, visionaries don't get sidetracked and integrators have a better-defined, more actionable set of responsibilities.

It takes only one question: *How does that align with our Absolute Focus?* If it doesn't, well, then I guess we won't be moving forward on it.

Now it's time to sit down and solidify your company's Absolute Focus. This is one of the hardest parts of WAVE. You are going to stick to this, and all of you will hold each other accountable, so it's important to get it right. But at the same time, you don't want to overthink it.

You want a very simple sentence or two that embodies *why* your company exists. It's a simple but impactful statement. It's bold and loud, and it comes from a pure place. It has nothing to do with money and everything to do with what you want your impact on the world to be.

This is your legacy … it's important to get it right. Be courageous. Be bold …

Here are some examples of Absolute Focus that I've worked on over the years.

Absolute Focus:

We exist to improve the lives of 100 million people by providing simple, effective products to solve irritating health challenges. We empower our customers to make smarter choices to heal themselves naturally.

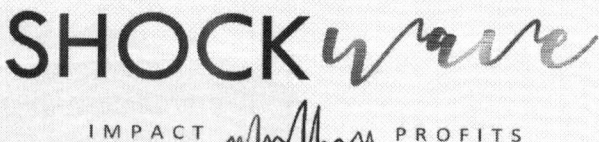

This company provides COO and Operations services.

Absolute Focus:
To guide visionary entrepreneurs to OPERATIONAL EXCELLENCE, PROFIT GROWTH & TALENT DEVELOPMENT

Pretty straightforward.

Once you have determined your Absolute Focus, here's a question to ask yourself: how does it align with your 10-Year Glimpse statement?

If the two don't vibe, you're off. Consider why they're out of alignment, and start again. What's causing the problem? How can you resolve it?

Your Absolute Focus should be your company's driving force, the reason it exists, and your 10-Year Glimpse should tell you exactly what you're driving toward. What's not in alignment?

Emma Rant:

Do not get discouraged if they are not aligned. Sometimes, drilling in is just part of the process, and that is TOTALLY okay. Stay the course. I promise, the work you put in now will pay off for years to come.

Far too often, this part of the process becomes an excuse for visionaries and/or integrators I've worked with. Not getting it perfect the first time does not mean that it was done wrong. It just means we need to spend more time on it.

Don't let your own limiting fears or alignment worries steer you away from this exercise. Drill down and dive in. Each time I've faced a Visionary/Integrator (V/I) duo, one of them wanted to abandon the process because of fear, anxiety, or frustration surrounding their own abilities.

It's okay to feel pressure here. In fact, LEAN INTO IT. Expose it for what it is: fear of moving forward. This is a very normal part of the process. You will expect your team to move forward when it's uncomfortable, so here is your chance to lead by example.

Your Absolute Focus should be descriptive enough that you can determine whether any hire, goal, task, product, or service aligns with it. Still, it should also be simple enough to say in a short sentence or two.

We are now halfway through WAVE, and by this point I usually feel pretty *accomplished*. The company's future and purpose are defined, while both visionary and integrator are aligned toward a common goal.

Now, it's time to think about what you truly value in your business.

Step 3: Values-Driven Future

In this step, we will be looking at the key values you want your team to have. You will hire, fire, promote, peer review, and mentor based on these four to six values.

That might sound a little extreme or too emotional, but that couldn't be further from the truth. Your values aren't about *liking* people. They're about making your business *work*.

Getting your team aligned means bringing in people who can be on the same page.

You don't want a team of yes-men who agree with everything you say (even if they really believe it), but when there's a fundamental clash in what different members of your team value, you're going to end up with conflicts and uncertainty.

Establishing your values means creating a base for your team and setting the grounds for success.

The first thing you want to do is think about two to three people you have worked with or for in the past and who you really admire. You know, when you are working with someone and you think, *Man, if I could clone so-and-so, we would really crush it.*

Now is your chance to do just that. Clone the people you like working with most by hiring them over and over again. In this exercise, you will jot down all of the main values these people brought to work, day after day. Make a list of elements you really enjoyed about them.

Here are some possibilities:

01.　　Truthful
02.　　Pride in Work
03.　　Aspire to Greatness
04.　　Integrity
05.　　Problem Solver
06.　　Action Taker
07.　　Grit
08.　　Lives in Awe
09.　　Empathetic
10.　　Energetic
11.　　Innovator
12.　　Collaborator
13.　　Team player

The list you make will likely have fifty or more words on it. Each person on your team that you've included in the WAVE process should make their own list.

Now, it's time to narrow them down. Make one master list; now, cross off all the words that have synonyms or that are requisites for other words on the list. For example, if you've listed honesty and integrity, you should cross off honesty and leave integrity, since you need to have the value of honesty to live with integrity.

Now, look through what is left, and circle all the words that resonate with you most. Keep working through this list until you have narrowed it down to four to six values.

Once you've finished, you'll have identified the values that will drive your future. You will utilize them for hiring, mentoring, promoting, and evaluating your staff.

Again, it's time to ask that question: do these values align with your goals for the future? With your Absolute Focus?

Furthermore, you must look at these values and ask yourself how they correspond with your leadership team. If your C-Suite and/or ownership do not possess these values, then you will either have to replace them or realign your values.

Emma Rant:

I've had visionaries insist on having a value on their list that they inherently do not have. They will argue with me that it is their opportunity to learn to be this way…

I will fight them to the death if needed. If YOU, as the CEO/ Owner/Visionary of the company, do not live in accordance with your own values, we've failed. Anyone on the team who fails to consistently demonstrate the values we've chosen will eventually be phased out of the business. You really need to think through that, yourself, and your people before solidifying your values list.

Step 4: Execute

WAVE is designed to help you write everything down and structure your business to align with your vision. You are getting everyone clear and empowering them to achieve that vision. If you do not execute, that vision is *just another dream*. It's all for nothing. That's a problem we've seen with *so many* consultants and businesses.

When I founded Shockwave, I knew I needed to solve a problem. I've seen far too many consultants come in, assist in creating the vision for a company they knew *nothing* about, and then just walk away.

Now, they may come back quarterly to check in on progress, but there's never any real path of execution. There's an end goal, but no map to get there. Sometimes, that's all that's needed, but in most cases, it leads to people falling short. The visionary, meanwhile, is left to look at their team like everyone failed or their vision isn't achievable.

Here is the reality: consultants who do not execute their own advice usually care only about how much you pay them. They may have great advice, but it's based on what you tell them in a short time. They have no real understanding of how your organization functions, and they have no discernment from an operational point of view on whether their advice is tangible.

This is why we at Shockwave put together a very specific Execution Plan to make the vision a reality. This encompasses how we communicate and how we move all these commitments forward.

We added a few key components to our business that allow us to stay on top of and hold all our team members accountable for keeping their commitments. We've successfully introduced those components to client after client.

Over the years, we've worked with many visionary-led companies in all aspects of internet marketing, so we had to devise a system that would take the vision and move it forward.

We needed an Execution Plan that didn't have bottlenecks and wouldn't leave us stuck. We have a guarantee to deliver on, after all. At Shockwave, we are the operations team. We do not walk away; we execute. So, our framework absolutely has to work.

So how do we Execute?

It's simple. It's a series of strategically placed goals, meetings, and follow-ups that keep things moving.

As you saw earlier in this chapter, the first thing we are going to do is set our One-Year Commitments, the five to fifteen goals that the business *will* accomplish this year. We may launch a new product line, add a key member, like a C-level executive, to our organization, or bring certain departments in-house.

No matter what they are, they need to be tangible and obtainable, but not easy.

We need to examine each goal and consider the resources we need to accomplish it. Once we have done that, we need to be honest with ourselves about whether we are truly willing to provide those resources.

Once we have identified the five to fifteen commitments we will accomplish, we need to dissect each and create a simple plan for them.

Who will be responsible for each one? Remember, we can have ONLY one person responsible for each one. Otherwise, you create a situation where everyone will point at everyone else if these projects don't get accomplished.

Once we know "who," we want to create a simple list of three to five milestones that must be achieved by the end of the year.

Look at your 3-Year Flash Forward, and ask yourself, *Will I be on track if I finish all these things in the next year?*

If your answer is yes, move on. If it isn't, let's keep going. What needs to be eliminated? What is a distraction? What needs to be added?

Now, you have your roadmap for the year. You know what your organization needs to accomplish over the next year to be on track for what we planned for years three and five.

The next thing we implement is a very structured quarterly meeting.

We will discuss the specifics of running this meeting later in this book, but basically, your company's quarterly meeting is a time for your team to do an end-of-quarter dissection. You will look back at all the wins and losses of the last quarter, spend time on team building, and create your goals for the next quarter.

This is a huge needle-mover for most businesses. It allows us to hyperfocus on a few projects and tasks each quarter, moving the company closer to its 10-Year Glimpse statement.

It is very important to create quarterly goals that stem from our yearly commitments. These are the milestones and needle-movers that drive the big picture.

We also have implemented a weekly meeting. Again, you can adjust this according to your needs. For some companies, it may make more sense to hold these bi-weekly, but the structure should be the same either way.

In any event, we call these Breakers. We gave it this name because a breaker is a wave whose amplitude (the energy contained in the wave) reaches a critical level, at which point major changes start to take place. In the ocean, this is where the wave changes from a swell to a crashing, stunning force.

In business, a Breaker is just as impactful, transforming day-to-day work into business-redefining events.

Breakers will *always* be at the same interval, on the same day, at the same time. We do not move them when the timing is inconvenient. We will take a deep dive into Breakers and how to run them in the last part of this book.

The next component to our Execution Plan is assigning what we call Movers to each person that can be accomplished from Breaker to Breaker. We don't set timelines across weeks or months, but simply from Breaker to Breaker.

Movers are the tasks that get us increasingly closer to achieving our quarterly goal. They are basically to-dos, but they relate right back to a specific quarterly goal. This will be discussed in Part Five of this book.

Finally, as part of the execution plan in WAVE, the visionary and integrator must be unified at all times in order to fully thrive as an organization. For that reason, we have come up with what we call unification meetings.

Travis and I do them as needed. I don't want us to get out of alignment and then wait for some monthly meeting on a calendar to address those things. We connect several times a week to make sure we are unified.

That said, your business probably doesn't need that much communication between your visionary/integrator duo. I will go more in-depth on this in Part Five of this book.

The very last part of the Execution Plan is that you create this one-page document I've spent so much time talking about.

Your WAVE is ready for a graphic designer who will create a one-page poster that encompasses your Written Vision, Absolute Focus, Values-Driven Future, and Execution Plan.

I've seen companies that took the time to build a vision but failed to execute on the one-pager part. But it's critical. It seems like such a minor thing, but it really makes a difference in implementing your vision with your team. Having this as a constant reminder keeps everyone rowing their canoes to the place they desire. Telling them that a map exists without giving them that map is about as useless as never creating the map in the first place.

Here's an example of what your WAVE might look like:

Next up… C

Part 2
Creating Processes

2.1 Why Creating Processes Is Important

Standard Operating Procedures are step-by-step instructions designed to help employees and vendors carry out routine operations.

Although everyday tasks often appear mundane and simple to experienced employees, they are much more complicated for new hires or people who are filling in.

You want the tasks you perform day in and day out to be clearly written, understandable, and repeatable. Some examples of these tasks are answering phone calls, issuing refunds, uploading content to social pages, hiring, using your business's tools and platforms, putting in a purchase order, monitoring inventory, categorizing charges in QuickBooks, and responding to customer complaints on the Better Business Bureau, etc.

You can see from the list that some of these tasks are imperative to running the business, and others are things that just need to get done.

Creating a set of instructions for every repeatable task ensures that your employees always meet industry standards, and that they understand the responsibilities of their positions.

Standard Operating Procedures improve the efficiency and effectiveness of an organization and simultaneously reduce threats of underperformance. Utilizing SOPs results in improved outcomes and shows demonstrable reductions in miscommunication.

Here are a few more reasons why SOPs are so important:

- They improve employee efficiency and company-wide communication.
- They reduce employee guesswork inefficiencies.
- They create a more consistent and cohesive work environment.
- They lower the risk of litigation.
- They ensure that operations comply with industry standards.
- They reduce costs.
- They increase productivity.
- They improve morale.
- They allow good employees to be sick or go on vacation stress-free.

Imagine you are on vacation and a key employee calls in sick due to an emergency. Think of all the things your team needs to accomplish during a normal business day. That might cause a whole vacation day lost for you. But if you have proper, documented SOPs in place, it will reduce a lost vacation day to perhaps an hour or two, if you need to spend any time on it at all. There's a world of difference.

Imagine a textbook filled with the steps everyone on your team takes to complete their tasks. Costs go down, because once you document the most cost-effective solution, you never have to worry about overspending.

Everyone knows how to perform that task in the most cost-effective way. This also makes hiring and training so much simpler. Imagine just being able to point someone to the right SOPs and have them take on their new responsibilities.

2.2 How to Create a Baller SOP

Every SOP has several must-have areas. I'll run through the essentials below; grab our template at <u>readscope.co/tools</u> for an instantly reproducible version.

The first is the SOP title. Clearly state what the SOP is for. That clarity is essential, especially when you have dozens of SOPs. An example would be:

How to Pull the Weekly Clockify Report

Next we add:

Date Created: Today's date

Created by: The person who wrote this up

Last Updated: The date of the latest update

Last Person to Update: Name of the person who updated

This will allow you to make sure your processes are being updated regularly—approximately once every six months—while maintaining a system for accountability. We should consistently explore the way our business does things and try to make it more efficient and cost-effective. This also gives employees ownership of their responsibilities, which generally causes buy-in.

Next should come a section that outlines the objective of the task. This will be broken into two parts: the Description and the Purpose of the process.

Description of the Process:

Pull a report from Clockify to verify and review hours worked by the employees.

Purpose of the Process Document:

Provide management with an overview of employees' hours.

Here we're explaining the task as simply as possible, then explaining *why* it has to be done. That's vital for onboarding, fill-in work, and employee buy-in.

Next is our Definitions section, which simply lists and defines any uncommon words or terms. This ensures that anyone who reads the document will understand what everything in it means.

Example:

Definitions

Clockify: A digital time clock where employees track their hours worked. They use it to clock in and clock out.

Next, you will type out the procedure. You may want to add screenshots or photos to help people understand the procedure. Each step should be written simply, just giving the facts about what needs to be done and any necessary context for the task.

Procedure

Note: This process is done on a weekly basis every Monday morning.

Step 1: Log in to Clockify.me.

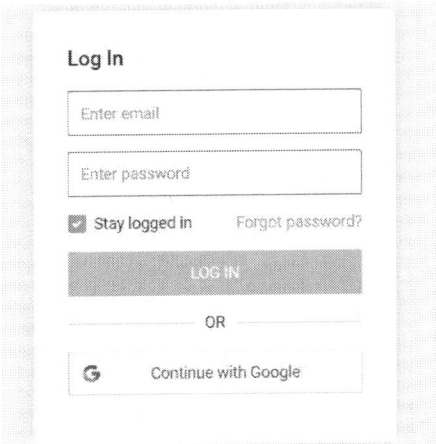

Step 2: Click on the Tracker tab – at the top left of the page.

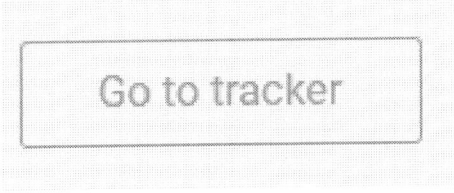

Step 3: Click on Reports.

Step 4: Click on Detailed – Highlight the last work-week dates on the calendar, and it will show up as "Last Week" at the top right.

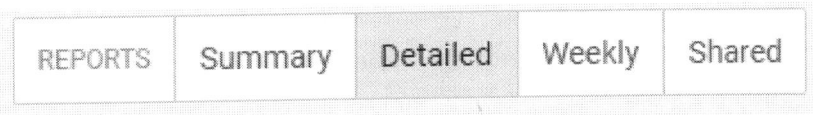

Step 5: Click on Teams.

Note: This report is only for hourly employees, and each individual employee will have their own report.

Step 6: Scroll down and click the name you want to report on, then click out of the selection area.

Step 7: Apply any necessary filter, and export – Save as PDF.

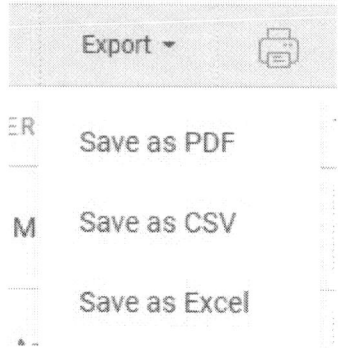

Step 8: Rename each PDF file with the individual's first name on the report, along with the end-of-week date (the Sunday, typically yesterday's date).

Step 9: Once finished, send all reports to the management team via email every Monday morning.

Once you've written out the process and included any necessary screenshots and photos, you may need to add a reference section. This can include extra documents that support the SOP, as well as links to websites and other related SOPs.

Then add a small section listing all the references (if any).

References

None

Finally, you want to insert contact information for one or two people in your organization who understand the task, so that the reader knows who to go to with questions or for clarifications.

Contact:

Emma Rainville

COO

Shockwave Solutions

emma@shockwavesolutionsllc.com

Weekly Clockify Report

Date Created: 11/25/2020
Created by: Emma Rainville
Last Updated: 11/25/2023
Last Person to Update: Emma Rainville

Overview

Description of the Process:
Pulling a report from Clockify to verify and review hours worked by the employees.

Purpose of the Process Document:
Executives want to make sure employees are not working unnecessary overtime.

Definitions

Clockify: A digital time clock where employees track their hours worked. They use it to clock in and clock out.

Procedure

<u>Note:</u> This process is done on a weekly basis every Monday morning.

Step 1: Log in to Clockify.me

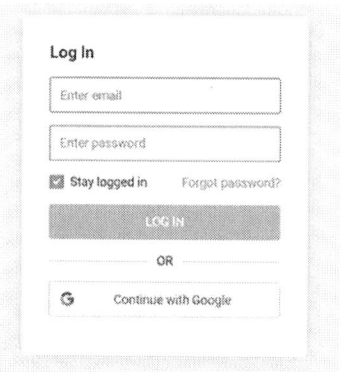

Step 2: Click on Tracker tab – top right of page.

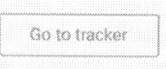

Step 3: Click on Reports.

Step 4: Click on Detailed – Highlight on the calendar the last work week dates and it will then show up as "Last Week" on the top right.

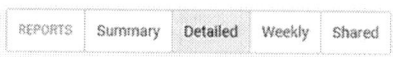

Step 5: Click on Team.

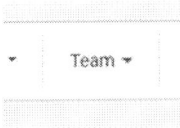

Step 6: Scroll down and click on each name you want to run in the report on and click out of that area.

<u>Note:</u> You will run this report with only the hourly employees. Each individual employee will have their own report. It is not done as a list of all employees together.

Step 7: Apply filter and export – Save as PDF.

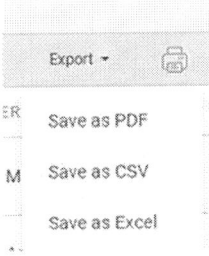

Step 8: Rename each PDF file with the individual's first name on the report with the Sunday date (before the next Monday of the upcoming work week).

<u>Note:</u> Follow Steps 2-8 to pull all individual reports.

Step 9: Once finished, send all reports to Emma Rainville via Skype or email every Monday morning.

Contacts

Emma Rainville
COO
Shockwave Solutions
emma@shockwavesolutionsllc.com

2.3 Overcomplicating Much?

Once you have a template and system for documenting process-es, the hardest part is not to overcomplicate the system.

You want to document tasks as simply as possible. You don't want to document things like how to shut the light off, how to check your email, or how to turn on your laptop.

Unless there is some intricate component to these things, do not write a process for them. If the whole world does the same thing in the same way, there is no reason to write out a process.

I once gave a little speech (Emma Translation: Mid-day rant) to a group of my employees. This was a new client's office staff, and I had spent about a week bonding as their new COO. In this speech, I started going on about how companies too often don't see the value in documenting processes, and how that is just irresponsible.

Then I left and went home for the night.

The next day I walked in, and these girls were all super excited to show me that they made SOPs. They were actually stoked to go through them so I could tell them what a great job they did.

Let me tell you, for a full minute I thought I must be on Candid Camera (I just aged myself), because they had written the most unorganized process documents on the silliest, most trivial things.

I shit you not, these girls wrote a document on when it was an appropriate time to use the restroom. It was so nuts, you can't make this shit up.

Another was where to get the bathroom key and how to unlock it. I really thought to myself for a moment that this has to be a joke. But then they proudly showed me the SOP for using Alexa... fucking Alexa...

I still cannot believe that happened. We ended up doing a lot of training, but eventually, people got the concept, and we created a written process for all appropriate tasks. It's really hard not to overcomplicate or over-detail the document.

2.4 Update, Then Streamline

At the same time, it can be easy to get lost in the details and make a complicated nightmare of a document. I remember one time when we were going to write the mother of all SOP documents. This SOP was going to have a full-on, step-by-step process that covered every single step to launching an offer—from picking, naming, and pricing the product, all the way to ramping up to launch Facebook ads.

This thing was not a process document. It was a *textbook*. It had processes that linked out to other processes that linked out to yet more processes.

I thought it was the most killer thing ever. Then I took it to the person who was my visionary at the time. I was so excited and proud when I handed him all forty-six double-sided pages. He looked at me and said, "What the fuck is this?" After I explained it and told him I'd shared the Google doc so he could link out to other pages, he said, "This is way too long. I'm not reading this shit."

He kind of threw it at me and then turned back toward his desk.

After I picked everything up off the floor, along with my pride, I realized it was actually way too long. No one was going to take the time to read anything that long.

I had not created a beautiful work of art, as I thought. Instead, I had created a long, drawn-out, ridiculous, and overcomplicated process that no one was ever going to read and (far more importantly) follow.

The point of an SOP is to simplify, and I had overcomplicated every step by "documenting" it.

For something as long and drawn-out as product launches, you want to make a checklist. Each item on the checklist may or may not need an SOP. Most of the tasks will probably need written processes, but they're not likely to be reviewed unless you break them down so that only the people performing them need to review them.

That particular full-launch process is now a one-page checklist containing three SOPs of about two pages each:

- An Operations SOP for launch
- A Marketing SOP for launch
- A Finance SOP for launch

Over time you get better at simplifying and effectively communicating processes. As you get better, so will your team. I, too, am still learning.

Essentially, think of the cogs in a clock. Things just somehow move and connect and keep everything flowing. That is how to think of SOPs. Place them where they need to go, and don't make them bigger than they need to be—or you'll find your clock grinding to a halt.

2.5 Creating and Updating SOPs

As I mentioned before, you want to review and update your processes twice a year. Allow yourself to be wrong, and welcome suggestions. Better, more efficient, and more cost-effective processes will be discovered if you constantly monitor your SOPs' impact.

When reviewing your SOPs, be sure to include all the people involved in completing that task. Ask them questions that can assist in determining if there are better ways to get the job done.

Employees who care can help maximize an organization's efficiencies by a very impactable amount.

As visionaries and integrators, we generally have a better understanding of how things work in our organization. Fine. But the whole reason we hire people is that they can do that job better than we can, or they have more time to focus on that component of the business.

So Let Them Do Their Job

The person who performs the task should be the one who creates and/or updates the SOP. That is not to say that we as leaders do not have something to say about the policy—we likely do—but don't assume you know better than the person doing the task.

If they've created a component of their SOP that you disagree with, it's far too easy to just tell them to change it. That will not create a good working relationship with them. You need to understand their why.

Without giving them any feedback, ask why they wrote the SOP like that. Understand their thought process and what challenges they faced that led them here.

Still don't agree with their procedure? Do you think you have a more effective way?

As executives, we often do. But the difference between bosses and leaders is that leaders will discuss and help *them* come up with the best practice. Do that, and you will get far more buy-in from them. They will be happy to make the changes if you come up with them together, rather than tell them how they are going to do things.

As a business owner, it is certainly your right to tell the people you pay how to do things. But you will get so much more out of your employees if you mentor them into doing things the most efficient way, rather than ordering them to do it "your way."

Part 3 -
Operational Excellence

3.1 Introduction to Operational Excellence

Operational excellence within the SCOPE framework reflects a strategic commitment to enhancing efficiency and effectiveness in every aspect of organizational operations. This pursuit not only ensures streamlined processes but also aligns with overarching business objectives that drive profitability and growth.

In achieving operational excellence, you must anticipate and mitigate issues related to growth. As businesses expand, the complexity of operations increases, making it crucial to proactively identify bottlenecks and challenges that could hinder progress. By optimizing efficiency through lean spending, organizations can allocate resources more effectively, ensuring that every dollar spent contributes to the overall strategy. This approach emphasizes the importance of consistent assessment and reallocation of resources to maintain effectiveness, avoid unnecessary expenses, and maximize ROI.

Developing the people within the organization is a cornerstone of sustaining operational excellence. As the business grows, so should its people. Investing in training and development ensures that existing teams can scale with the company, which reduces the need for costly new hires. A culture of continuous improvement and learning not only enhances employee engagement and retention, but also builds a workforce capable of driving the business forward, maintaining the delicate balance between growth and operational efficiency.

Operational excellence is not a one-time achievement; it's an ongoing journey. It requires a comprehensive approach that integrates foresight, resource optimization, and talent development, ensuring that the organization remains agile, resilient, and poised for sustained success.

There is nothing about operational excellence that is sexy. It doesn't carry the same excitement or hype as marketing, but this is where you go from making money to *keeping* money. I've found throughout my time at Shockwave Solutions working with many different businesses that most of them figure out how to get revenue through the door, but they get stuck on how they keep it at the end of the day.

The major pain points tend to be the daily fires that spark up on a day-to-day basis, usually because of poor planning and operational inefficiencies. For example, many of the owners we've worked with have no idea what their profit margin is. They are clueless about their run rate[3] or even what that means, and they are unclear on inventory or even how the delivery process in their business works. Those things aren't "sexy," but they're essential to running a business.

---

3   Run Rate is the predicted revenue of a company for the year, extrapolated from a particular period. As an example, to calculate a Run Rate based on results from June, you'd take the total revenue from June, divide it by the number of days in the month (thirty), then multiply by 365 for your annual Run Rate. While an effective shorthand for prediction, it's important to factor in additional circumstances to make Run Rate a more trustworthy predictor. For example, fitness businesses typically see their highest revenue numbers in January—a Run Rate based on January would give an inaccurate prediction for annual revenue.

The unsexy parts of your business are where the "kept money" comes from, so let's spend some time understanding what that is and how it runs in a healthy, profitable business where we respond to fires because we anticipated them, rather than reacting and blowing our plans for the day completely.

3.2 Operational Excellence and SCOPE

Operational excellence within the SCOPE framework is more than just a set of practices—it's the cornerstone of sustainable business success. It represents a disciplined, strategic approach to systematically enhancing every facet of company operations, ensuring that the organization is not only efficient, but also resilient and adaptable in the face of growth.

At its core, operational excellence begins with a relentless focus on continuous assessment and improvement. This means regularly evaluating processes, identifying inefficiencies, and implementing solutions that streamline workflows, reduce waste, and enhance overall quality. But it doesn't stop there. SCOPE emphasizes the importance of foresight—anticipating potential challenges that come with growth and addressing them before they become obstacles. This proactive stance ensures that the organization remains agile and capable of scaling without losing momentum or compromising its strategic goals.

Moreover, operational excellence within SCOPE is driven by a commitment to resource optimization through lean practices. Every dollar spent and every resource allocated are scrutinized to ensure maximum return on investment. This minimizes unnecessary costs and redirects resources to areas that directly contribute to the company's long-term objectives. It's about doing more with less—achieving greater efficiency without sacrificing quality or effectiveness.

A crucial yet often overlooked aspect of operational excellence is the development of the organization's people. SCOPE recognizes that as the business grows, its people must grow with it. Investing in employee training and development is not just a nice-to-have; it's a strategic imperative. By cultivating the skills and capabilities of existing teams, the organization can scale effectively without the need for constant hiring, which can be costly and disruptive. This approach fosters a culture of continuous improvement and empowerment, where employees are not just participants but drivers of the company's success.

In essence, operational excellence within the SCOPE framework is about building a business that is not only profitable, but also sustainable, scalable, and aligned with its long-term vision. It's about creating an operational foundation that supports growth, fosters innovation, and positions the organization as a leader in its industry. This commitment to excellence is what differentiates successful companies from those that struggle to keep pace in a rapidly changing business environment.

3.3 Impact on Profitability and Growth

Operational excellence is not merely a tool for improvement; it is a critical driver of both profitability and sustainable growth. Businesses can maximize resource utilization by systematically minimizing waste and eliminating redundancies, leading to significantly lower operational costs and higher profit margins. This efficiency isn't just about cutting costs—it enhances the organization's overall financial health, ensuring that every dollar spent is aligned with strategic objectives.

Growth, often accompanied by increased complexity, is made more manageable through the principles of operational excellence. Scalable and efficient operations allow businesses to handle larger volumes and expanded markets without compromising quality and performance. This scalability is essential in competitive markets, where the ability to grow without sacrificing operational integrity is a decisive factor in long-term success.

By embedding operational excellence into the core of the SCOPE framework, businesses lay a solid foundation for sustained efficiency and profitability. This approach not only supports immediate financial gains but also ensures that the organization is equipped to thrive in an ever-evolving market landscape.

3.4 SCOPE Principles in Modern Operations

Management by Objectives

Setting Clear, Achievable Goals: We focus on setting clear goals that are Specific, Measurable, Achievable, Relevant, and Time-bound (SMART). This approach ensures that all team members know exactly what is expected and can measure their progress against defined objectives.

Here are two examples:

Example 1: Increasing Monthly Sales Revenue

Goal: Increase the monthly sales revenue by 15 percent over the next quarter.

- **Specific:** The goal is to increase sales revenue.
- **Measurable:** The target is a 15 percent increase in revenue.
- **Achievable:** Based on past performance data and current market conditions, a 15 percent increase is realistic with additional marketing efforts and sales training.
- **Relevant:** Increasing sales revenue directly contributes to the company's growth and profitability objectives.
- **Time-bound:** This goal is to be achieved over the next three months.

Objective: The designated team member will target an additional $5,000 in sales per month by focusing on upselling to existing clients and reaching out to new leads generated by the marketing department.

Example 2: Reducing Customer Support Response Time

Goal: Reduce the average customer support response time to under four hours within the next sixty days.

- **Specific:** The goal is to reduce the response time for customer support.
- **Measurable:** The target is an average response time of under four hours.
- **Achievable:** With the implementation of new support software and additional training, this reduction is feasible.
- **Relevant:** Faster response times improve customer satisfaction and retention, aligning with the company's customer service excellence goals.
- **Time-bound:** This goal is to be achieved within sixty days.

Objective: Each support team member will be trained on the new software, and performance will be monitored weekly to ensure response times are decreasing progressively.

3.5 Monitoring and Feedback

Regular reviews and feedback sessions are cornerstones of the SCOPE framework. They ensure that all goals remain aligned with the overall operational strategy and that necessary adjustments are made promptly. In this approach, the primary tool for these reviews is the Breaker, a ninety-minute weekly meeting dedicated to evaluating progress toward quarterly goals (we will go in depth on the Breaker later in the book).

During each Breaker, team members present their progress on goals, detailing the specific actions they've taken over the past week to move closer to achieving these objectives. This structured review allows for a clear assessment of whether goals are on track and helps identify any potential challenges early on.

If questions or issues arise regarding any goal, they are added to the Signals list—a key component of the Breaker. The Signals list acts as a queue for addressing challenges where the entire team can collaboratively brainstorm solutions, provide constructive feedback, and adjust strategies as needed. This process fosters a culture of continuous improvement and ensures that all team members are supported in reaching their goals.

By integrating regular reviews and feedback sessions through Breakers, the SCOPE method guarantees dynamic and responsive goal-setting, enabling the team to adapt to changes and maintain alignment with the company's broader strategic objectives.

3.6 The Role of Innovation and Entrepreneurship

3.6.1 Innovation as a Driver

Innovation is not just an added value; it is a fundamental driver of operational excellence. In today's rapidly evolving business landscape, the ability to innovate is crucial for streamlining workflows, enhancing productivity, and staying ahead of the competition. By embedding innovation into the very fabric of the organization, we transform it from a periodic effort into a continuous, ingrained practice that propels the company forward.

Fostering a **culture of innovation** means creating an environment where every team member feels empowered to think creatively, challenge the status quo, and contribute to the development of new processes, products, and solutions. It's about making innovation a core expectation, where continuous improvement is the standard, not the exception.

For example, I've worked with a team that regularly holds Innovation Sprints—dedicated time blocks where employees are encouraged to explore new ideas, test unconventional solutions, and prototype innovations without the usual constraints of their daily responsibilities.

One such sprint led to the development of an automated task management system that reduced project turnaround times by 30 percent. This system, born out of a culture that values and nurtures innovation, not only streamlined operations but also significantly boosted productivity across the board.

By cultivating this culture of innovation, we ensure that the organization remains agile, capable of adapting to new challenges, and consistently improving its operations. This approach enhances immediate productivity and builds a robust foundation for sustained growth and long-term success. Innovation, when treated as a continuous driver, becomes the engine that powers the entire organization toward excellence.

3.6.2 Entrepreneurial Mindset

Cultivating an entrepreneurial mindset within our teams is not just a strategy—it's a competitive advantage that sets Shockwave apart in a crowded marketplace. An entrepreneurial mindset fosters a culture of proactive problem-solving, where team members are empowered to take initiative, think creatively, and develop innovative solutions to operational challenges. This mindset goes beyond simply reacting to issues; it encourages foresight and the anticipation of market shifts, enabling the organization to stay ahead of the curve.

By embedding this mindset into our daily operations, we create a workforce that is agile, adaptable, and capable of swiftly responding to changing market dynamics and evolving customer needs. This is crucial in today's fast-paced business environment, where the ability to pivot quickly and effectively can mean the difference between leading the market and falling behind competitors.

Moreover, this entrepreneurial approach is deeply rooted in structured, modern operational practices. By anchoring our operations in proven management theories while maintaining a forward-thinking outlook, we ensure that our strategies are both grounded in experience and poised for success. This balance between stability and innovation is what drives Shockwave's operational excellence, leading to sustained growth and profitability.

In essence, an entrepreneurial mindset is the catalyst for continuous improvement and strategic advantage. It empowers our teams to not only meet challenges head-on, but to turn those challenges into opportunities for growth, ensuring that Shockwave remains at the forefront of its industry.

3.7 Creating a Culture of Productivity

Establish a culture of transparency and open communication where employees feel safe to express ideas, concerns, and feedback. This openness promotes a healthy work environment and encourages innovation and problem-solving, which enhance operational efficiency.

3.8 Collaboration and Teamwork

Collaboration and teamwork are not just encouraged at all the companies I've been the COO for—they are fundamental to our success. By facilitating opportunities for employees to work together on projects, we foster a culture where diverse skills and perspectives converge to create innovative solutions. This collaborative environment enhances problem-solving and strengthens the sense of belonging among team members, making everyone feel like an integral part of the company's journey.

Take, for example, Richard and Saka from Shockwave Solutions' marketing team. They frequently collaborate on funnel building[4]

---

4   Funnel building is an essential part of eCommerce. A funnel isn't just a way for customers to buy the products you're selling; it's an evolving environment designed to bring in revenue at all stages, from pulling in customers to your email list all the way through to upselling buyers on additional programs and products. Funnel building involves continual testing, iteration, and optimization to maximize results.

and split testing[5] projects. By combining Richard's expertise in analytical skills with Saka's sharp digital marketing strategy, they are able to design and optimize marketing funnels that consistently outperform expectations. Their collaborative efforts have led to significant increases in lead conversion rates, driving more targeted traffic through our sales processes and directly contributing to revenue growth.

Another powerful example of teamwork at Shockwave is the partnership between Emma and Daniel. Emma, with her deep understanding of operations, and Daniel, who leads the customer service department, work closely to transform customer interactions into revenue-generating opportunities. By aligning customer service strategies with broader revenue goals, they've developed a system where customer inquiries and feedback are not just resolved, but also leveraged to upsell services and build stronger client relationships. This collaboration has turned our customer service department into a key revenue stream, further solidifying Shockwave's market position.

Then there's the dynamic duo of Nelson and Jay, who edit our videos to create viral moments that seamlessly lead back to Emma and Travis' podcast, *Special Ops*. Their collaborative synergy is evident in the way they craft visually compelling stories that resonate with our audience, driving engagement and boosting the podcast's reach. By aligning their creative talents, they ensure that every piece of content not only entertains but also serves as a strategic touchpoint for our brand's message.

These examples demonstrate how collaboration at Shockwave is more than just working together—it's about harnessing the collective strengths of our teams to achieve exceptional results. By

---

5   Split tests are a method used in marketing and product development to compare two versions of a variable to determine which performs better. This testing approach is often used to optimize marketing strategies, website designs, or product features by randomly dividing the audience into two groups and exposing each group to a different version. The results are then analyzed to decide which version yields better results in terms of conversions, user engagement, or other key metrics.

encouraging teamwork and providing platforms for cross-depart-mental collaboration, we tap into the full potential of our diverse skill sets. This not only accelerates problem-solving, it also drives innovation, efficiency, and a deeper connection to the company's mission.

In essence, collaboration and teamwork are the engines of our operational excellence—and should be at the heart of yours. By leveraging the unique abilities and perspectives of each team member, we ensure that our projects are not only successful, but also impactful, contributing to sustained growth and a strong company culture.

3.9 Improving Productivity and Engagement

Growth for employee productivity and engagement is driven by two key factors: autonomy and recognition. By integrating these principles into our daily operations, we create a workplace where each team member feels valued and empowered, leading to both individual and organizational success.

3.9.1 Employee Autonomy

Granting employees autonomy over how they manage their work-load and solve problems is fundamental to fostering a sense of responsibility and ownership. For instance, I've mentioned above how Richard and Saka operate within the marketing team. They are given the freedom to design and execute their funnel-building and split-testing strategies, allowing them to explore creative solutions without micromanagement. This autonomy drives their motivation and leads to innovative approaches that enhance our marketing efficiency and effectiveness.

Similarly, Nelson and Jay, our video editors, are empowered to take charge of their creative process. They are given long-form content, and then they decide how best to edit and produce con-tent that will create viral moments. This freedom to innovate has led to a series of highly engaging videos that significantly boost the podcast's reach and, in turn, our brand's visibility.

3.9.2 Recognition and Appreciation

A critical component of enhancing productivity and engagement is an unwavering commitment to recognition and appreciation. I've implemented a peer recognition system that allows teams to acknowledge each other's contributions and successes openly. This approach has proven particularly effective in fostering a supportive and collaborative work environment.

One of the ways we've embedded this practice into our culture is through the Breaker. Each meeting begins with a few prompts, one of which has team members sharing what they are grateful for. This simple yet powerful practice provides an opportunity for staff to express their appreciation for each other's efforts, whether it's help with a project, a shared success, or simply support in day-to-day tasks.

For instance, Richard might express gratitude for Saka's assistance in a project he was running late on, or Nelson might thank Jay for his creative input that enhanced a video edit. This regular exchange of appreciation both boosts morale and strengthens the bonds within the team, driving everyone to maintain high performance standards.

By integrating these practices into our operations, we cultivate a culture where productivity and engagement are the natural outcomes of employee empowerment and mutual appreciation. Our approach ensures that all team members feel valued and motivated to contribute their best, knowing their efforts are recognized and impactful. This focus on recognition not only enhances individual performance but also drives the overall success of the organization, solidifying Shockwave's position as a leader in its industry.

3.10 Process Optimization

Achieving operational excellence within any organization hinges on the strategic integration of modern technology and an unwavering commitment to continuous improvement. These elements are not just complementary; they are essential for transforming how a company operates, ensuring it remains competitive and agile in a rapidly evolving business landscape.

3.10.1 Technology Integration

The integration of advanced technology into daily operations is a critical driver of efficiency and effectiveness. By embracing cutting-edge tools and systems, companies can automate repetitive tasks, enhance data accuracy, and significantly speed up decision-making processes. This transformation is not just about keeping pace with technological advancements; it's about leveraging these innovations to optimize every facet of the organization's operations.

For instance, implementing AI-driven analytics tools can revolutionize how a company identifies and addresses operational bottlenecks. These tools can analyze vast amounts of data in real time, providing deeper insights into areas where processes may be slowing down or where resources are being underutilized. By pinpointing these issues, businesses can make targeted improvements that lead to substantial gains in productivity and efficiency.

Consider a manufacturing company that adopts predictive maintenance systems. These AI-driven systems monitor machinery and equipment in real time, predicting potential failures before they occur. This proactive approach to maintenance minimizes costly downtime and reduces the need for expensive emergency repairs, directly contributing to the bottom line. The result is a smoother, more reliable production process that keeps operations running at peak efficiency.

In the realm of customer service, technology integration can take the form of sophisticated CRM systems that track customer interactions across multiple channels. These systems can automatically categorize and prioritize customer inquiries, ensuring that high-priority issues are addressed swiftly while providing agents with all the information they need to resolve problems effectively. This leads to faster response times, higher customer satisfaction, and, ultimately, increased loyalty and revenue.

3.10.2 Continuous Improvement

While technology provides the tools for optimization, a culture of continuous improvement ensures that these tools are used to their fullest potential.

Adopting a kaizen approach—where small, incremental changes are made consistently over time—cultivates a mindset of ongoing enhancement across the organization.

Continuous improvement begins with empowering employees at all levels to identify opportunities for refinement. This could involve regular brainstorming sessions where teams come together to discuss potential process improvements, no matter how minor they may seem. For example, in a customer service department, a team might suggest a simple change in how calls are logged, resulting in more efficient handling of customer data and a reduction in call times.

A commitment to continuous improvement is embedded in our operations. Teams are encouraged to review their workflows regularly, identify inefficiencies, and propose solutions. For example, a marketing team might collaborate on refining its funnel-building process, incorporating feedback from split tests to enhance conversion rates. This iterative approach improves outcomes and fosters a sense of ownership and pride in the work being done.

Moreover, continuous improvement isn't limited to operational processes. It extends to the development of products, services, and even corporate culture. By regularly assessing and refining every aspect of the business, companies can adapt more quickly to changes in the market, meet customer demands more effectively, and stay ahead of competitors.

Integrating technology with a commitment to continuous improvement forms the backbone of process optimization. When these elements are harmonized, they create a powerful engine for operational excellence. Technology provides the tools to automate, analyze, and accelerate, while continuous improvement ensures that the organization remains agile, responsive, and consistently moving forward. This robust approach not only enhances efficiency and productivity but also drives long-term growth and success, positioning the organization as a leader in its industry.

I have an expectation that all team members review their SOPs twice a year to see if there are improvements that can be made either in efficiency or through new technology.

3.11 Decentralization and Decisions

3.11.1 Decision-Making and Risk Management

In today's rapidly evolving business landscape, the ability to make timely and informed decisions is a critical determinant of success. As organizations grow and markets become more complex, the principles of decentralized decision-making and proactive risk management become not just beneficial but essential. I'm going to explore how decentralizing decision-making empowers mid-level managers to drive operational excellence and the strategies necessary to align risk assessment with organizational goals, ultimately enhancing performance and stability.

3.11.2 Decentralizing Decision-Making

Decentralizing decision-making is a strategic approach that shifts authority from upper management to those closer to the action. By empowering mid-level managers to make decisions, organizations can respond more rapidly and effectively to operational challenges. This approach not only enhances efficiency but also fosters a culture of innovation, agility, and customer-centricity that is crucial for thriving in today's fast-paced business environment.

3.11.3 Benefits of Decentralization

Increased Agility: Decentralization significantly boosts an organization's agility by enabling faster decision-making at the operational level. When authority is distributed closer to the point of action, managers can quickly respond to changes in the market or internal challenges without waiting for approvals from higher-ups. This speed is crucial in industries where conditions can change rapidly, allowing the organization to seize opportunities and mitigate risks in real time.

Enhanced Innovation: Empowering managers to make decisions encourages them to think creatively and take initiative. When managers have the freedom to experiment, it opens the door to innovative solutions that might not emerge in a more rigid, centralized structure.

For example, a marketing manager who is reviewing our split test data day-to-day is far more likely to pick a winning split test experiment than an executive who isn't seeing what is winning on a day-to-day basis. The person responsible for handling the task and getting their hands dirty is far more equipped than someone like me. Though my experience far outweighs theirs, their consistent presence in the department makes them more knowledgeable.

Improved Customer Engagement: Decentralized units typically have closer contact with customers, which allows for a more tailored and responsive approach to customer service. Managers who are on the ground can quickly adapt products, services, or processes to meet specific customer needs, leading to higher customer satisfaction and loyalty.

For instance, a customer service team empowered to resolve issues immediately, without escalating to higher management, can turn potentially negative experiences into positive ones, thereby enhancing overall customer engagement.

3.11.4 Empowering Mid-Level Managers

Effective decentralization requires mid-level managers to have the skills and knowledge they need to make informed decisions. Visionaries should invest in comprehensive training programs that focus on critical areas such as strategic thinking, financial analysis, and leadership.

For example, training programs could include simulations where managers practice making decisions in various scenarios, or workshops that cover best practices in risk management and resource allocation. These programs should also emphasize the importance of aligning decisions with broader organizational goals to ensure consistency and coherence across the company.

Emma Rant:

When I started offering a training program for lower-level managers called Operations and Leadership Training, I did so because so few companies in Direct Response and eCommerce mentor and offer training for their people, yet they expect them to grow with the company. It is important to provide the tools your loyal people need to grow with you.

When evaluating training programs, you should look for courses that include:

Scenario-based learning: This allows managers to practice decision-making in simulated environments, preparing them for real-world challenges.

Cross-functional collaboration exercises: These help managers understand the impact of their decisions on different parts of the organization.

Leadership development modules: Focus on building the confidence and skills necessary to lead teams effectively while making autonomous decisions.

Offer live classes or office hours. Watching modules will not have nearly the same impact as live courses and opportunities to interact with the other students and instructors.

Clear Guidelines and Accountability

Decentralization doesn't mean a free-for-all. It's essential to establish clear guidelines that define the scope within which managers can operate. These guidelines should outline the parameters of their decision-making authority, including budget limits, strategic priorities, and risk tolerance.

Additionally, establishing accountability mechanisms ensures that managers understand their responsibilities and the consequences of their decisions. Regular reviews and performance metrics tied to decision outcomes can help maintain alignment with the company's strategic objectives. Remember, you cannot hold someone accountable if you have not adequately explained expectations. I will usually have my staff and manager repeat to me what they believe the expectation is, so we both are clear on what the other person has said.

Support Systems

To ensure that low- to mid-level managers are not isolated in their decision-making roles, organizations must provide robust support systems. This includes access to real-time data, which empowers managers to make informed decisions based on the latest information.

Additionally, offering senior advisorship—where managers can consult with experienced leaders when facing particularly complex or high-stakes decisions—ensures they have the guidance they need to navigate challenges effectively. For instance, a manager in charge of a product launch might have access to market analytics and customer feedback in real time, along with the ability to consult with a senior executive to refine the launch strategy.

Decentralizing decision-making is a powerful strategy that, when implemented effectively, can transform an organization's operational efficiency, innovation capability, and customer engagement.

By empowering mid-level managers with the tools, training, and support they need, organizations can create a more agile, responsive, and innovative workforce. This approach not only accelerates decision-making processes but also ensures that decisions are made by those who are closest to the action, leading to more relevant and impactful outcomes. Through thoughtful implementation of decentralization, businesses can position themselves to adapt swiftly to change, capitalize on new opportunities, and maintain a competitive edge in their industry.

3.12 Risk Management Strategies

Effective risk management is a cornerstone of operational excellence. A dynamic process that involves identifying, assessing, and managing potential risks to minimize their impact, it ensures that organizations can navigate uncertainties while continuing to achieve their goals.

By integrating robust risk management strategies into the fabric of daily operations, organizations can proactively mitigate threats and sustain long-term growth, especially in the fast-paced world of direct response online selling.

Comprehensive Risk Assessment Audits

Conducting regular risk audits is crucial for maintaining a comprehensive understanding of the risks that may affect an organization, particularly in the dynamic environment of online selling. This goes for both direct response marketers and eCommerce sellers. These audits should be systematic and thorough, covering all aspects of the business, from digital marketing strategies to supply chain logistics and data security.

For example, an online retailer might conduct quarterly risk audits focused on key areas such as website performance, payment processing reliability, and the effectiveness of marketing campaigns. A risk audit could reveal that a significant portion of the retailer's traffic is coming from a single digital ad campaign, posing a risk if that campaign underperforms or is paused. In response, the retailer might diversify its marketing channels to reduce dependence on any single source of traffic.

To effectively carry out a risk audit in a direct response online selling business:

- **Step 1:** Identify the scope of the audit. This might include areas such as website uptime, payment gateway performance, customer data security, and fulfillment operations.

- **Step 2:** Gather data through analytics tools, customer feedback, and operational reports. For instance, using analytics tools to track website performance and identify potential bottlenecks.

- **Step 3:** Analyze the data to identify potential risks, such as a slow-loading website or frequent cart abandonment at the payment stage.

- **Step 4:** Evaluate the potential impact of each identified risk, prioritizing those that could have the most significant effect on sales and customer satisfaction.

- **Step 5:** Develop and implement mitigation strategies, such as optimizing website speed, securing alternative payment gateways, or enhancing customer support during high-traffic periods.

3.12.1 Stakeholder Involvement

Involving various stakeholders in the risk assessment process ensures that all potential risks are considered from multiple perspectives. In the context of an online business, this could mean engaging digital marketers, IT professionals, customer service teams, and even third-party logistics providers.

For example, when launching a product, the marketing team might identify risks related to ad performance and customer acquisition costs, while the IT team would highlight concerns about website traffic surges and server capacity. By bringing these insights together, the business can create a more robust plan that addresses both marketing and operational risks.

Proactive Risk Management Integration

Risk management should be an integral part of daily operations rather than a separate, reactive activity. By embedding risk management into the organization's operational processes, risks can be identified and mitigated in real time.

For instance, an online seller might integrate risk management into their email marketing campaigns. If an email campaign is generating unusually high traffic to the website, the business can proactively scale server resources to handle the increased load, preventing website crashes that could lead to lost sales. Similarly, regularly monitoring customer feedback on social media and review sites can help identify emerging risks to the brand's reputation, allowing the business to address negative sentiments before they escalate.

3.12.2 Technology Utilization

Leveraging technology is essential for enhancing the effectiveness of risk management strategies. Advanced tools such as AI-driven analytics, predictive modeling, and real-time monitoring systems can help online sellers identify emerging risks.

For example, an online retailer could use predictive analytics to forecast inventory needs based on historical sales data and upcoming promotions. This allows the business to mitigate the risk of stockouts or overstock situations, both of which can have a significant impact on profitability.

Additionally, using AI to monitor customer behavior patterns can help identify potential fraud, enabling the business to take preventative measures.

Building a Culture Around Risk Awareness Training

Implementing training programs focused on risk awareness and management equips employees at all levels with the skills they need to recognize and address potential risks. In an online business, these programs might cover areas such as cybersecurity, data privacy, and customer service escalation protocols.

For instance, a training program for the customer service team could include modules on identifying phishing attempts or handling data breaches. Similarly, the IT team might undergo training on the latest cybersecurity threats and how to mitigate them. By equipping employees with this knowledge, the business ensures that potential risks are recognized and managed before they can escalate into significant issues.

When developing a training program for an online business, consider:

- **Content Relevance:** Ensure the training addresses the specific risks relevant to the employees' roles, such as cybersecurity for IT staff or fraud detection for customer service teams.
- **Engagement:** Use interactive methods like simulations or real-world scenarios to make the training more engaging and effective.
- **Assessment:** Include post-training assessments to gauge understanding and retention of the material.

3.12.3 Open Communication Channels

Encouraging open communication about risks is vital for fostering a proactive risk management culture. Employees should feel comfortable discussing potential risks and vulnerabilities without fear of blame, or you run the risk of never identifying issues until they start having a negative impact.

For example, a customer service representative at an online retail business might notice an increase in complaints about delayed shipments. Instead of keeping this information to themselves, they should feel empowered to raise the issue with the operations team, which can then investigate and address the underlying problem. This open communication helps prevent minor issues from developing into major disruptions.

Emma Rant:

Far too often, staff on the ground see things before they are issues. If we do not teach them to ring all the alarms and report what they see, and then reward them for finding issues and bringing them to our attention, we risk valuable time—or worse, depending on the situation.

I once was the COO of a fitness giant, and one of the customer service manager's tasks was to go through all the links to all the sales pages on a daily basis and to test every page and upsell. Once she was done, she would sign her initial to show she walked through the funnel.

One evening I received a call from one of our offshore, after-hours CS agents who noticed the upsell pages were not loading after the purchase. The funnel randomly just ended. It was a three-second tech fix, but the CS manager who checked the funnel in the morning did not report it.

The next day I asked her why she just put her initials on the sheet without checking the funnel. She replied, "I did check the funnel before I initialed the sheet." After a few minutes of questions, I realized that letting someone know it was broken was not in the SOP. That seemed like common sense to me...but it obviously didn't to her.

This taught me a great lesson: make sure that SOPs, particularly those that exist to prevent risk, are spelled out in detail.

Continual Improvement of Risk Management

Establishing mechanisms to gather feedback on the effectiveness of risk management strategies is essential for their continual improvement. This could involve regular surveys, focus groups, or feedback sessions with employees and stakeholders.

For example, an online seller might gather feedback from their team after a major campaign to assess what risks were encountered and how they were managed. If the campaign experienced issues like ad fatigue or delivery delays, this feedback can be used to refine future strategies, such as diversifying ad creatives or improving supplier communication.

3.12.4 Learning from Past Incidents

Analyzing past incidents and their management responses provides valuable insights that can inform future strategies. Online businesses should maintain detailed records of incidents such as website outages, payment processing failures, or inventory shortages, and conduct thorough reviews to understand what went wrong and how similar risks can be mitigated in the future. This is not in place to assign blame, and in fact you never should. Its sole purpose is to create an SOP that never allows the same incident to come up again in your business.

For instance, if an online seller experienced a significant drop in website traffic due to a Google algorithm update, analyzing the incident could reveal gaps in their SEO strategy. The business could then adjust its content and link-building tactics to be more resilient against future updates, ensuring a more stable flow of organic traffic.

By embracing decentralized decision-making and integrating comprehensive risk management strategies, direct response online sellers can achieve a higher level of operational excellence. This approach not only empowers mid-level managers to act decisively, it also aligns the entire organization toward a common goal of sustainable growth and resilience against potential threats. Regular risk audits, proactive management, a culture of risk awareness, and continual improvement are the pillars that support this robust strategy. They ensure the organization remains agile, resilient, and competitive in the fast-paced world of online selling.

3.13 Decision-Making and Risk Management: Measuring Operational Success

In the pursuit of operational excellence, the measurement of success is as critical as the strategies and processes implemented to achieve it. This section delves into the metrics and Key

Performance Indicators (KPIs) essential for evaluating operational health and the effectiveness of management strategies, particularly through the lens of operational excellence.

Understanding Metrics and KPIs

Metrics and KPIs are the quantifiable measures used to track and assess the efficiency and effectiveness of various operations within an organization. These indicators are not merely numbers—they are vital tools that provide insights into how well the organization meets its operational goals and objectives. The right metrics and KPIs help leaders make informed decisions, drive continuous improvement, and align day-to-day operations with strategic goals.

Selection of Metrics and KPIs

Relevance

The chosen metrics must align directly with the organization's goals. For example, if the goal is to enhance customer satisfaction, relevant metrics might include customer service response time, Net Promoter Score (NPS), and repeat customer rate. These metrics provide a clear picture of how well the organization is meeting customer expectations and where improvements can be made.

Clarity and Simplicity

Metrics should be straightforward and easily understandable to ensure they can be monitored and acted upon effectively. Complex or ambiguous metrics can lead to confusion, misinterpretation, and ultimately ineffective decision-making. For instance, instead of tracking abstract indicators, focusing on clear, actionable metrics like "order fulfillment time" or "error rate in billing" ensures that everyone in the organization understands what is being measured and why it matters.

Timeliness

Metrics should be available in real time to allow for quick decision-making and adjustments. In fast-paced industries, delays in accessing performance data can result in missed opportunities or unresolved issues that escalate into bigger problems. Real-time metrics, such as website uptime or daily sales figures, enable organizations to respond swiftly to emerging trends or disruptions, maintaining operational agility.

Effectiveness Metrics

Effectiveness metrics focus on how well the organization is achieving its desired outcomes. These metrics help assess the success of marketing campaigns, customer engagement, and overall sales performance.

Examples include:

- **Conversion Rate:** The percentage of website visitors who complete a desired action, such as making a purchase or signing up for a newsletter. A higher conversion rate indicates that marketing efforts and website design are effectively driving customers to act. This metric is crucial, as it directly correlates to sales performance.

- **Customer Lifetime Value (CLV):** This metric estimates the total revenue a business can expect from a single customer over the course of their relationship. CLV is vital for understanding the long-term profitability of customer acquisition strategies. A higher CLV suggests that the business is not only attracting customers but also retaining them through effective follow-up marketing and excellent customer service.

- **Average Order Value (AOV):** AOV measures the average amount customers spend each time they place an order. Increasing AOV, often achieved through upselling and cross-selling strategies, should be a key goal for most businesses.

Monitoring AOV helps businesses understand customer purchasing behavior and optimize pricing strategies.

- **Cart Abandonment Rate:** The percentage of shoppers who add items to their cart but leave the site without completing the purchase. A high cart abandonment rate indicates potential issues with the checkout process, pricing, or shipping options. Reducing this rate can significantly increase sales and improve overall effectiveness.

- **Email Open and Click-Through Rates:** For direct response marketers, the effectiveness of email campaigns is crucial. The open rate measures the percentage of recipients who open an email, while the click-through rate (CTR) measures the percentage of recipients who click on a link within the email. High rates suggest that the email content is engaging and relevant, driving traffic back to the website or landing pages.

- **Return on Ad Spend (ROAS):** ROAS measures the revenue generated for every dollar spent on advertising. It's a critical metric for direct response marketers as it directly links marketing efforts to financial returns. A high ROAS indicates that the advertising strategy is cost-effective and successful in driving sales.

3.13.1 The SCOPE Approach to Effective Management

SCOPE's approach to management effectiveness is rooted in transparency, agility, and continuous improvement. This approach transcends the maintenance of standard operations and pushes the boundaries of what can be achieved through innovative practices and technologies.

Integrating Real-Time Data Analysis

Incorporating real-time data analysis into operations allows for immediate insights and swift decision-making. For example, by utilizing advanced analytics platforms, we can monitor customer interactions on our sales pages in real time and adjust marketing strategies, pricing, or customer service approaches instantly to optimize conversion rates and enhance the customer experience.

Employee Engagement Metrics

A highly engaged workforce is a highly productive one. We closely monitor metrics like employee satisfaction, engagement scores, and turnover rates. By analyzing these metrics, the company can identify areas where employee morale might be lagging and take steps to address these issues, such as by offering additional training, improving workplace culture, or providing incentives.

Innovation Rate

Innovation Rate is a metric that measures the frequency of new ideas or improvements implemented within the organization. This might be tracked by the number of new product features rolled out, the introduction of process improvements, or the adoption of new technologies. A high Innovation Rate indicates a dynamic, forward-thinking organization that continuously evolves to meet market demands.

For instance, if someone in your organization introduces five new automated tools for their customer service process in a quarter, this would reflect a strong Innovation Rate, showcasing the company's commitment to enhancing efficiency and customer satisfaction through innovative solutions.

Flexibility Index

The Flexibility Index is another key metric, assessing the organization's ability to adapt to changes without significant performance loss. This might measure how quickly an organization can pivot its marketing strategies in response to shifting consumer trends, or how effectively the supply chain adapts to disruptions.

For example, during a sudden surge in demand for a particular product, an ability to scale up production and distribution without delays or quality compromises would contribute to a high

Flexibility Index. This metric reflects the organization's resilience and capacity to thrive in a volatile market.

Evaluating Operational Health and Effectiveness

Operational excellence is not a static state, something you can achieve and then stop thinking about; it's a constant process of improvement. The true test of operational excellence lies in the continuous evaluation and recalibration of processes based on the insights derived from key metrics.

Regular monitoring and adjustment ensure that your organization's operations remain aligned with strategic objectives and can respond effectively to internal and external challenges.

Regular Reviews and Adjustments

Regularly scheduled reviews of operational metrics are essential for ensuring that deviations from expected performance are caught and addressed promptly. You may choose to review on your Breaker weekly or monthly, depending on the metric, and involve cross-functional teams that analyze the data, discuss findings, and implement necessary adjustments.

Continuous Feedback Loops

Creating mechanisms for constant feedback allows for ongoing adjustments, ensuring operations remain aligned with strategic objectives. For instance, customer feedback collected through surveys or social media monitoring can be used to make real-time adjustments to marketing campaigns or product offerings, maintaining a strong connection with the market and customer base.

The Role of Metrics in Strategic Decision-Making:

Integrating well-defined metrics and KPIs into the management strategy is a game changer for maintaining and enhancing operational excellence.

SCOPE's approach, which combines innovative practices with a solid foundation of risk management and decision-making frameworks, exemplifies how modern metrics can drive an organization toward unprecedented levels of success and sustainability.

By continuously measuring and analyzing these metrics, organizations not only ensure their operations are running smoothly but also foster an environment of perpetual growth and improvement. This metrics-driven approach empowers the executive team or ownership to make strategic decisions that are informed, timely, and aligned with long-term goals, solidifying its position as a leader in the industry.

3.14 Building a Learning Organization

In our rapidly changing business world, fostering a culture of curiosity and experimentation is essential for staying ahead of the curve. This involves creating an environment where employees are encouraged to ask questions, explore new ideas, and view challenges not as obstacles but as opportunities for growth. The traditional mindset of maintaining the status quo must be replaced with a proactive approach that values innovation and continuous improvement.

To cultivate this culture, organizations should:

- **Implement Regular Learning Sessions:** Conduct workshops, seminars, and brainstorming sessions that go beyond the immediate needs of team members' roles. For example, a direct response marketing company might organize a session on the latest trends in AI-driven customer insights, even if it's not yet a core part of the business. This broadens employees' understanding of the industry and sparks new ideas for applying emerging technologies to current challenges.

- **Encourage Cross-Departmental Collaboration:** Promote projects where employees from different departments collaborate to solve complex problems. For instance, the marketing team could work with the IT team to develop a more effective customer segmentation tool, combining creative strategies with technical expertise. This not only drives innovation but also helps employees appreciate the diverse skills within the organization.

- **Empower Employees to Experiment:** Provide the necessary resources and time for employees to test new ideas. For example, allow the marketing team to run small-scale A/B tests on new campaign strategies without needing extensive approvals. By making it safe to fail, you encourage a mindset where learning and improvement are the primary goals.

Leveraging Technology to Enhance Learning

Technology is a powerful enabler of continuous learning and development, offering tools that can make education more accessible, personalized, and effective. By leveraging online platforms and learning management systems, organizations can provide a wide array of learning resources tailored to individual needs.

- **Utilize Online Learning Platforms:** Platforms like Coursera, LinkedIn Learning, and company-specific Learning Management Systems can offer employees access to courses that fit their learning styles and schedules. For example, an eCommerce business might use these platforms to offer courses on advanced digital marketing, allowing employees to learn at their own pace.

- **Employ Analytics for Tailored Learning:** Use data analytics to track learning progress and adapt educational content to meet specific developmental needs. For instance, if analytics reveal that employees struggle with data analysis, the organization can introduce targeted workshops or additional training modules to close this gap.

- **Virtual Simulations and Gamification:** Incorporate simulations and gamified learning experiences to make complex concepts more engaging. For example, a customer service training program might include a virtual simulation where employees must handle difficult customer interactions, providing them with practical experience in a risk-free environment.

Aligning with Business Objectives

Aligning training programs with business objectives ensures that the investment in employee development directly contributes to the organization's success. This alignment helps employees see the tangible impact of their learning on the company's goals, thereby increasing motivation and engagement.

- **Link Training to KPIs:** Design training programs that are directly tied to Key Performance Indicators (KPIs). For example, if a KPI is reducing customer churn, training could focus on improving customer service skills or enhancing product knowledge. This makes it clear how training contributes to achieving strategic business goals.

- **Operational Role-Based Training:** Develop training modules based on specific operational roles to ensure that the skills learned enhance both efficiency and effectiveness in those roles. For instance, a logistics company might create a training program for warehouse staff focused on inventory management and efficient order fulfillment processes, directly improving operational performance.

Developing Future Leaders

Preparing for the future involves identifying and nurturing the next generation of leaders within the organization. Leadership development should be an ongoing process, supported by mentorship and targeted development programs.

- **Mentorship Programs:** Establish mentorship programs where less experienced employees are paired with seasoned leaders. This facilitates knowledge transfer and helps mentees develop the skills and confidence needed for leadership roles. For example, a high-potential junior marketer might be mentored by a senior marketing executive, learning not just technical skills but also strategic thinking and decision-making.

- **Succession Planning:** Implement succession planning programs that identify high-potential employees and provide them with the training needed to assume leadership roles in the future. This could include rotational programs where employees gain experience in different departments, preparing them for broader responsibilities. For example, a promising IT manager might rotate through finance and operations to build a well-rounded skill set.

Continuous Improvement Through Employee Feedback

Feedback is a critical component of any learning and development program. By continuously gathering and acting on employee feedback, organizations can refine their training programs to better meet the needs of their workforce.

- **Develop Feedback Loops:** Create mechanisms for employees to provide regular feedback on training programs. These could include surveys, focus groups, or informal check-ins. For example, after rolling out a new sales training module, ask participants for feedback on its relevance, content quality, and applicability to their daily work.

- **Example of a Feedback Loop:** At an eCommerce company, a feedback loop was established for a new customer service training program. Initial feedback revealed that employees found the content too theoretical and not directly applicable to their work. The company responded by incorporating more practical exercises and real-world scenarios into the program. As a result, employee engagement increased, and turnover rates decreased significantly, demonstrating the power of responsive training design.

3.15 Overcoming Challenges to Learning Organizations

Training in a fast-paced, constantly evolving industry presents unique challenges. Organizations must ensure that training remains relevant, adaptable, and aligned with ever-changing business needs.

- **Aligning Training with Industry Changes:** One of the biggest challenges is keeping training programs up to date with the latest industry trends and technological advancements. To overcome this, organizations can adopt agile training methodologies. For example, instead of annual training updates, introduce micro-learning sessions that can be quickly adjusted to reflect new developments. This could involve biweekly webinars on the latest eCommerce tools or emerging digital marketing techniques.

- **Measuring the ROI of Training Programs:** Another challenge is proving the return on investment (ROI) of training programs, particularly in a dynamic environment where results may take time to manifest. Organizations can address this by integrating real-time feedback systems and data analytics to track the impact of training on performance metrics. For instance, by correlating training completion rates with sales performance data, an online retailer can demonstrate the direct effect of sales training on revenue growth.

Reiterating the Value of Continuous Learning

The importance of continuous learning cannot be overstated in a rapidly developing environment. Organizations that prioritize learning as a strategic imperative are better equipped to adapt to change, foster innovation, and achieve long-term success.

- **Strategic Importance of a Learning Organization:** Building a learning organization means embedding continuous learning into the core of the company's operational strategy. This requires commitment from leadership and a culture that values knowledge sharing, experimentation, and continuous improvement.

For example, our operations team at Shockwave Solutions integrates continuous learning into daily operations through regular learning sessions, collaborative projects, and a robust feedback system that ensures learning is aligned with business objectives. This gives them an "unfair" advantage when taking over operations for our clients. They are always one step ahead of the average person that you might hire.

- **Direct Correlation Between Learning and Success:** Continuous learning has a direct impact on employee satisfaction, operational excellence, and overall business success. Employees who are encouraged to learn and grow are more engaged, innovative, and committed to the organization's goals. For example, by investing in ongoing training for customer service representatives, an eCommerce company can enhance the customer experience, leading to higher customer retention rates and increased revenue. For every dollar you put into growing your team, you will typically receive three times that in cost savings and additional efficiency.

- **Example:** A growing online retailer, facing increasing competition, decides to invest heavily in continuous learning. They introduce a series of advanced analytics training sessions for their marketing team, enabling it to better understand customer data and refine targeting strategies. Over time, this investment in learning leads to a significant increase in conversion rates, demonstrating the direct link between continuous learning and business success.

By addressing challenges head-on and fostering a culture of curiosity, innovation, and continuous learning, organizations can create a resilient, adaptable workforce capable of navigating the complexities of today's business environment. The path forward is one of empowerment—giving employees the power to think critically, innovate boldly, and take ownership of their development and the company's success.

Through strategic training and development aligned with business objectives and supported by real-time feedback, organizations can achieve not only operational excellence but also long-term sustainability and growth.

3.16 Harnessing Operational Excellence for Sustained Success

In our exploration of operational excellence, we've delved into the core strategies that serve as the foundation for sustained business success. This chapter has woven together essential elements such as continuous improvement, decentralized decision-making, technological integration, risk management, metrics-driven performance, and the cultivation of a learning organization. These strategies are not standalone efforts; they are interconnected pillars that, when integrated, create a resilient and adaptable organization capable of thriving in a dynamic business environment.

Embracing a Culture of Continuous Improvement

Throughout this chapter, we've emphasized the need to foster a culture where innovation and efficiency are continuously pursued.

By encouraging employees to engage in problem-solving and process optimization, organizations can keep pace with changing demands and capitalize on new opportunities. Regular training, a steadfast commitment to quality, and the use of innovative practices and technologies are the bedrock of this culture. For example, Shockwave Solutions regularly conducts workshops that challenge employees to rethink existing processes and propose new solutions, creating a culture of perpetual improvement.

Decentralizing Decision-Making

Empowering mid-level managers and front-line employees with decision-making authority has emerged as a crucial strategy for maintaining agility and responsiveness. This decentralization both accelerates operational responses and fosters a sense of owner-ship and responsibility among employees. By granting autonomy, organizations like Shockwave Solutions ensure that decisions are made closer to the point of action, leading to more informed and timely outcomes. This approach has the added benefit of enhanc-ing employee engagement, as team members feel more directly connected to the success of the organization.

Integrating Advanced Technologies

The integration of cutting-edge technologies such as AI, machine learning, and data analytics has fundamentally transformed how businesses operate. These tools provide critical insights and fore-sight, enabling organizations to predict market trends, streamline operations, and personalize customer experiences at unprec-edented scales. By adopting these technologies, companies can not only improve efficiency but also unlock new avenues for growth and innovation. Shockwave Solutions, for instance, has leveraged AI-driven analytics to optimize their customer segmen-tation strategies, resulting in more targeted marketing campaigns and higher conversion rates.

Prioritizing Risk Management and Resilience

Risk management is not a reactive measure; it's a proactive strategy that must be woven into the fabric of every organizational process.

Throughout this chapter, we've highlighted the importance of identifying, assessing, and mitigating potential disruptions before they can impact operations. By integrating risk management with operational processes, companies can shield themselves against potential losses and capitalize on unforeseen opportunities. For example, Shockwave Solutions conducts regular risk audits that allow the organization to adapt quickly to market changes, ensuring both stability and agility.

Measuring Success Through Metrics and KPIs

The role of metrics and KPIs in operational excellence cannot be overstated. These tools are essential for gauging the health and effectiveness of operations. By setting clear, measurable objectives aligned with strategic goals, organizations can track progress, make informed decisions, and drive continuous improvement. Throughout this chapter, we've underscored how Shockwave Solutions uses metrics like conversion rates, profit margins, and customer satisfaction indices to monitor performance and refine strategies in real time, ensuring alignment with broader business objectives.

Building a Learning Organization

Continuous learning and development are the cornerstones of long-term success. As operational demands evolve, so too must the skills and knowledge of the workforce. By committing to ongoing education, organizations ensure they remain competitive and prepared for future challenges. A learning organization is one that fosters curiosity, encourages experimentation, and supports the professional growth of its employees.

Operational excellence isn't a finish line—it's a relentless journey. We've dissected the core elements that fuel this journey and contribute to a framework designed for long-term success.

Central to operational excellence is smart decision-making and proactive risk management. By pushing decision-making down the ranks and empowering managers, you create a more agile organization. This agility is key to navigating market shifts, seizing opportunities, and tackling threats head-on. Routine risk audits and real-time data ensure your decisions are sharp, informed, and aligned with your strategic goals.

Metrics and KPIs serve as the backbone of continuous improvement. By homing in on efficiency and effectiveness metrics specific to direct response and eCommerce, you gain a clear view of your organization's health.

Regularly reviewing these numbers allows you to make decisions that enhance everything from customer conversions to profit margins, but operational excellence isn't just about processes and numbers—it's about culture. When you foster a culture of curiosity, innovation, and ownership, your employees don't just do their jobs—they drive your business forward. Encouraging your team members to challenge the status quo and constantly learn turns them into active contributors to your growth.

Training and development must evolve with your business. Aligning training with your goals and leveraging technology ensure your team is always ahead of the curve. Continuous feedback and adaptive training reinforce your organization's ability to thrive, no matter what the future holds.

But here's where the rubber meets the road: Operational excellence isn't worth a damn without the right people to execute it. You can have the best processes in place, but if your team isn't on board, you're dead in the water. The culture you cultivate—one of curiosity, accountability, and constant learning—determines whether your organization will just survive or actually thrive.

This is where people development takes center stage. It's not a nice-to-have; it's a must-have. The same rigor you apply to refining your operations needs to be applied to developing your team. Align training with your strategic goals, leverage technology for smarter learning, and make sure every employee is not just a cog in the machine but an active participant in your growth.

Now, as we transition from operational excellence to the people who make it happen, remember this: Your operations are only as good as the people who run them. So, let's dive into how to develop a workforce that doesn't just keep up but leads the charge.

Part 4 -
People Development

4.1 Why It's Important to Put A Solid Team in Place

The primary purpose of people development is to align individual growth with the overarching objectives of your organization, growing both your team and the individual people within it. By investing in your people, you ensure that every team member not only understands their role in the company's vision but is also equipped to execute it effectively.

This alignment is crucial for fostering a sense of ownership and engagement among staff, which directly influences productivity and the achievement of business targets.

Many leaders underestimate the immense power of building a talented and diverse team that shares values and vision—a strong and cohesive team of people who are not afraid to debate each other, who you can trust to keep things moving in the direction of the vision you've created, and who have the potential to take you to extraordinary heights that were once unimaginable, either solo or with a non-aligned team.

Collectively, a well-formed team has incredible strength. The ability to leverage this to overcome challenges and previous limitations is an indicator of exceptional leadership.

Far too often, leaders can become bottlenecks for their own businesses, preventing them from growing and progressing. People development means stopping this pattern, giving team members the ability to step up and complete projects, and empowering them to lead in their own right.

Without development, we fall short of our potential and fail in our responsibility as leaders.

In Part One, we talked about establishing our values, one of the crucial parts of team development. Now let's take this a little further.

In business, particularly in direct response, we often spend many man-hours understanding our demographic and building an avatar for our perfect customer.

Ever think why we we're not spending the time to create an avatar for our perfect employee?

MIC DROP, RIGHT?

When we are working on a marketing campaign or a series of split tests, we need to know the kind of person we're targeting. Messaging is a bit easier when you imagine the person you are talking to and know how they think and will respond.

That imagined person becomes your avatar, your ideal customer. With this avatar in place, understanding how to shape your offers becomes drastically simpler. You know what your avatar wants, you know their pain points and how to address them.

In a lot of ways, creating an employee avatar is similar. We're aiming to understand our ideal candidate and learn how they'll fit in with our existing team.

Step one of creating your employee avatar comes with the Values-Driven Future portion of your WAVE instructions. You need to understand the values that underpin your business and how to look for those values when hiring.

Even if someone is the most talented applicant, I won't hire them if their values don't align with those of the company. Even if I believe they have the potential to generate millions of dollars, I refuse to compromise our company's values.

This would jeopardize all the effort I've put into assembling a dynamic team that functions like a well-oiled machine—a team that engages in healthy debates, works together for the greater good, and supports each other in achieving goals and strategies that aren't strictly their own responsibilities.

The saying, "One bad apple spoils the bunch," holds true for teams as well. One unproductive team member can drag down the entire team's ability to complete projects. On the other hand, one highly productive team member can significantly boost productivity across the entire company. I've witnessed this firsthand in my own business and in the businesses of my clients throughout the years.

Emma Rant:

I find it frustrating when I am working with a visionary who constantly complains that "no one can keep up with them." This is usually because they have not spent the time they need to build a team, share the vision in a way that their staff can understand, or create plans or projects with reasonable expectations. Because they are unable to lead, they blame staff members, who are often left feeling underpaid, underappreciated, frustrated, and without purpose.

Once we've decided to hire for a role, we build a hiring sheet that makes the avatar clearer and more detailed. This one-page document describes what the person we are onboarding will be responsible for, what expectations we have of them, and what KPIs they have to hit at thirty days, ninety days, and 180 days.

Sometimes, opportunities come when we are least prepared for them. While it's important not to miss out on great opportunities, such as finding the perfect candidate, just because you weren't actively seeking them, it's also crucial to take the time to plan for the long term. Although focusing on the present is often fine, it's essential to enter a situation with a solid plan. Providing your candidate with every opportunity to succeed will result in a higher return on investment for that hiring decision.

In this section, I'll guide you through the entire process, from hiring and onboarding to development and mentoring.

4.2 Hiring SOPs and Tips

Too often, we hire based on our first impressions in an interview, but I've found value in hiring individuals I didn't personally like, yet who perfectly matched our values and culture.

Their personalities didn't resonate with me, but their skills and their alignment with my company's values were undeniable. If they meet every requirement, does my personal opinion really matter?

Separating personal bias from hiring decisions can significantly benefit your organization.

Maybe the job applicant has a loud laugh or makes an irritating noise when drinking, but what truly matters is whether they can contribute to our team and our collective goals. My personal preferences should take a backseat to the criteria I've set out.

Interestingly, every time I've hesitated to hire someone because I didn't like their personality, I've ended up appreciating our relationship within three months. This has happened without fail.

Those who follow my blog posts or podcasts might recall my assistant, Julie. Initially, I disliked everything about her, yet she became an invaluable part of my team.

My business partner, Travis...

I hated him on our first call. Now he is my lifelong best friend. I absolutely love that man.

My point is not to hire based on feelings; hire based on ability.

So, let's dive into Shockwave's hiring process. Now, I am not saying you need to follow my process 100 percent, but I am saying you *must* have a process. You can adjust mine to fit your preferences and then follow it like it's the law every time.

Here are our steps:

Step 1: Once a position opens, the HR Coordinator sends PrevueHR test invites to potential candidates.

Step 2: Candidates complete the PrevueHR test, which assesses their logical reasoning and personality fit for the role.

Step 3: The HR Coordinator reviews test results against the benchmarks set for the role and selects candidates for an initial interview.

Step 4: The Director of Operations/Chief of Staff conducts a fifteen-minute preliminary interview to filter candidates based on professionalism and any immediate deal-breakers.

Step 5: Successful candidates from Step 4 are scheduled for a ninety-minute, in-depth interview with the CEO or relevant manager that focuses on company values and situational problem-solving.

Step 6: During the in-depth interview, candidates are also assessed through a practical test to evaluate their proactive problem-solving skills.

Step 7: Post-interview, the CEO/Manager discusses the candidate's potential alignment with our culture and expectations, reviewing long-term goals and operational fit.

Step 8: If a candidate meets all criteria, the HR Coordinator organizes a final evaluation session to discuss the specifics of the role and the company's expectations, and to clarify any final questions or concerns.

Step 9: Once a candidate is approved, the HR Coordinator sends an offer letter. Upon acceptance, the candidate is briefed on their start date and onboarding process.

Step 10: The Director of Operations/Chief of Staff coordinates the onboarding schedule and ensures that the new hire is equipped with the necessary resources and is introduced to key team members.

Step 11: The new hire begins their role, with initial tasks designed to integrate them into the team and familiarize them with Shockwave's operational protocols.

Let me go over some of the whys on this SOP so you can understand the order.

The reason I make potential candidates take the PrevueHR test before they talk to anyone is that Shockwave is a vicious animal. I mean that. We are coming into companies that are completely *fucked*. I have been described as a lion, pit bull, and grizzly bear.

While I do hate that, the fact of the matter is that it is absolutely true.

If a business is bringing in millions of dollars but is not holding on to its profits, something is broken. Someone needs to come in and sort it out fast, and that is what Shockwave does.

Our staff often has to move at the rate of insanity. That requires people who can problem-solve, think for themselves, have extreme ownership accountability, and come up with strategies. But it also requires that they move when told, without asking questions. We can dissect all of it later so they can learn.

I need to haul ass sometimes, so my team—my whole team—has to be willing to run and jump off a cliff with me and have total trust that the water will be deep enough when they hit it.

Guess what.

They all have that trust. While it takes some time to get there, if you are the type of person who needs to have an in-depth phone call before you take a test for your interview...

You are none of the things I just described. In a major way, taking the test is the first test I give a candidate.

I have chosen PrevueHR as my candidate-testing platform because it reveals the things I want to know. I don't care what a candidate actually knows. If they are coming into direct response, they don't know shit; they have to be taught. (There is hardly anyone running real ops in our sector, so it is highly unlikely that anyone would come in with any direct experience.)

PrevueHR uses two sections—a series of logic puzzles covering core competencies and a wide range of personality questions. Here's what we see at the end:

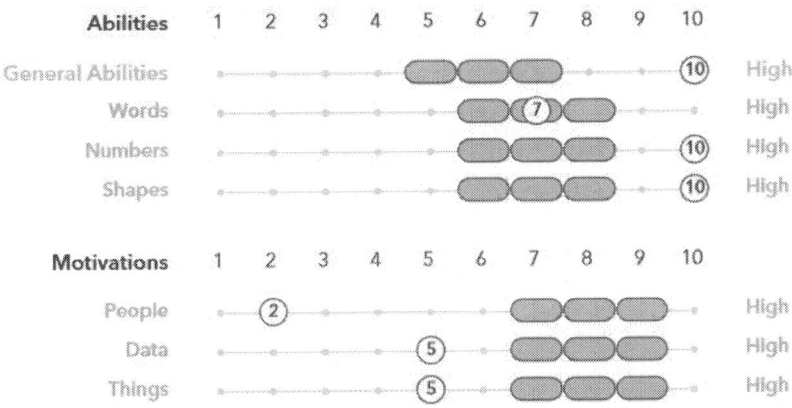

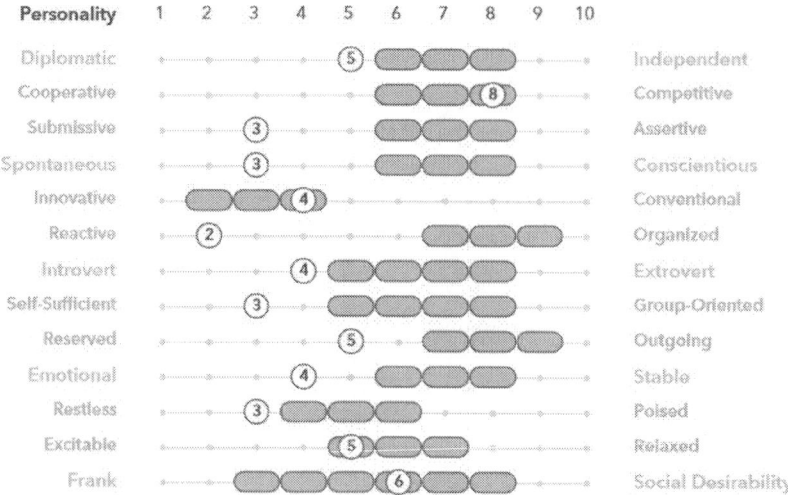

Personality	1	2	3	4	5	6	7	8	9	10	
Diplomatic					(5)						Independent
Cooperative								(8)			Competitive
Submissive			(3)								Assertive
Spontaneous			(3)								Conscientious
Innovative				(4)							Conventional
Reactive		(2)									Organized
Introvert				(4)							Extrovert
Self-Sufficient			(3)								Group-Oriented
Reserved					(5)						Outgoing
Emotional				(4)							Stable
Restless			(3)								Poised
Excitable					(5)						Relaxed
Frank						(6)					Social Desirability

It explores a person's ability to learn tasks and their interest in working in those categories. I don't care that you scored a ten in working with numbers. If your interest in it is a two, it will never work.

PrevueHR looks at a job-seeker's specific personality and allows you to set benchmarks for comparing their scores with the expectations of the job, both in terms of responsibility and personality, seeing where they excel, and where they may fall short.

I typically set these benchmarks by giving the test to two or three people who are doing the same or a similar job well. I then use their average scores to determine where potential candidates should sit.

As an example, if you are hiring a customer service representative and their interest in working with people scores a two out of ten, then they probably shouldn't be the person your customer talks to.

Most companies test a person's capability but often fail to match those skills with their interest in the role and whether their personality is compatible with the job.

If I decide that the candidate is suitable for a full-on interview, I'll add another level of testing. I ask specific questions based on missed benchmarks. If I require someone to be organized, and their personality test shows them to be disorganized, that does not mean they don't recognize that. If they know there's a problem and they have contingencies in place to make up for it, that changes everything.

I am insanely disorganized as a human being. I score a two, meaning I'm reactive rather than organized. But if someone asked me the question that PrevueHR automatically suggested for my personality type, my explanation would make them feel completely comfortable.

Most people I work with have no idea that I am so disorganized. I have highly organized team members all around me and lots of intentional structure, so it's never an issue. The PrevueHR test allows for explanation and exploration, because EVERYONE will fall short in some way. The point is to find the best match, not the perfect match.

Next, my director of operations or my chief of staff does a fifteen-minute interview. As I said earlier, I don't care if I like someone. But certain things are just a no-go; they scream immediate stop for me.

Let me give you some examples:

If a candidate can't get dressed for a Zoom call, I'm not interested.

If there are cats or dogs running around in the background during an interview, I know client calls will be a nightmare.

If there's a trashed room in the background or empty liquor bottles lined up behind the candidate, I'm not interested.

If they are smoking or drinking on the call…

All of these have actually happened. There are probably fifty more things I can add, but you get the idea.

Once they get past my Director of Operations or Chief of Staff, they have a ninety-minute interview with me and/or Travis, depending on the role/situation.

In this ninety-minute interview, I tell them about our company values and ask them to give me an example of something they did or a situation they were in within the last month where they displayed the values we're looking for. I am asking for real, actionable implementation for the specific value. We want to be sure the person lives up to the avatar.

For example, one of our values is that every team member must be a proactive problem-solver.

I want humans who can assess risk and prevent problems before they become problems. I want to hear a story about someone who was able to determine an issue and mitigate it through proactive problem-solving.

It can be as simple as:

I noticed that my tire was a little low, so I brought my car in to make sure it wasn't an issue.

Or, I noticed a spill at the grocery store, so I had my daughter get an employee to clean it up while I stood by to alert people and make sure no one slipped.

If you value that, it will be who you are even when you're not at work.

Once I've reviewed all our values, I start asking the questions about where they fell short of my avatar for the role according to the PrevueHR test.

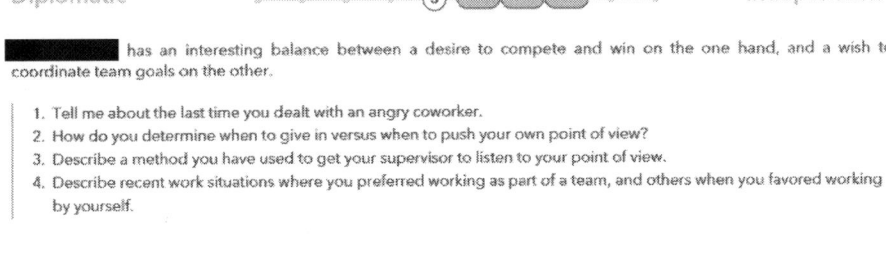

Diplomatic   1 2 3 4 5 6 7 8 9 10   Independent

███████ has an interesting balance between a desire to compete and win on the one hand, and a wish to coordinate team goals on the other.

1. Tell me about the last time you dealt with an angry coworker.
2. How do you determine when to give in versus when to push your own point of view?
3. Describe a method you have used to get your supervisor to listen to your point of view.
4. Describe recent work situations where you preferred working as part of a team, and others when you favored working by yourself.

If I like their answers and decide to move ahead, I have a list of further questions for a deep dive. You can grab that list by visiting readscope.co/tools.

Just as there is more than one way to skin a cat, there are lots of ways to ask the same question. You'll see that some of the questions are the same or similar, but they are worded differently. I choose the exact wording based on how I'm communicating with the candidate in the interview.

I go through the questions and see if the candidate aligns with me, or with Shockwave, or with the company I am hiring for. Do they align with our avatar? Are they going to fit in and improve the flow of operations, or will they present a challenge?

I ask about their long-term goals. Mainly, I am watching for certain language that tells me they put a lot of thought into their personal and professional goals. Operations needs people who are three steps ahead of everyone else, and they can't be if they don't plan everything. People who don't take the time to plan out their own lives aren't going to do a good job planning for my clients.

One of the things I do that hands-down *wins* for me every time is pretending to lose my keys.

This works only with in-person interviews, but you can get creative over Zoom if necessary.

Here's what I do: During the entire time that I'm asking the questions listed on readscope.co/tools, I act as if I'm looking for something. But I say nothing. I just shuffle things around, making it obvious that I am looking for something and stressing about it.

Some people will just sit there. It won't bother them at all.

Some will get stressed and distracted but say nothing.

I'm looking for people who say, "What are you looking for?" and then start helping.

Not every rock star will be that bold, so if they don't ask you anything, say to them, "Do you see any keys over there?"

If they look side-to-side and say no, I cut them loose. While my team and I are struggling, they will clock out at 4:30. These will not be problem-solvers or team players. Even a tech hire should want to help me in a small way. Remember, my number one core value is a proactive problem-solver. So someone who will comfortably sit by and watch me struggle isn't for me.

I was super annoyed by one applicant I was interviewing. She answered all the questions correctly, but she laughed awkwardly at everything and sort of sang a few of her answers.

I hired her anyway, because she found my keys in my purse. This girl had no issue jumping up and searching relentlessly through everything until she found them. I wasn't going to ask her one more question, and she wasn't leaving until we found these keys.

She was in the top five hires of my career.

The test here isn't only resourcefulness, it's also personality. Are they fine watching someone drown right in front of them? Do they care about only what they need to accomplish and provide?

You can be the best at what you do, but if you are not a team player, if you have a "me" over a "we" mentality, I don't want you.

In the last part of the interview, I like to discuss who I am as a person and a boss. My expectations for Shockwave employees are enormous. Every time they speak to a client, they take that information as if it came directly from me. I do not like failing to meet expectations. My reputation for dependability is very important to me. I get anxious just thinking about my staff not delivering on something they said they would.

In my opinion, whether you are in an interview or on a first date, we need to be completely honest with each other. I don't like breakups, so let's avoid them by being exactly who we were on day one. I'm not going to try to persuade you that this is a dream job, that you'll get tons of time off, never work nights or weekends, and that I'm the nicest person on planet earth.

Nope, I'm going to tell you exactly what you are going to get. We are ride-or-die for our clients. If there is any trouble, we have our hands in all of it.

Shockwave is a consulting agency, but we come in as a COO and ops team. So if a regular COO and ops team would be dealing with broken links at 2 a.m. on a Saturday, you can damn well bet that we will be too.

Sometimes my expectations are above what a normal human is capable of. That's why I do not hire normal humans. My level of loyalty is unmatched on this earth, but yours had better be too. I can be completely unreasonable—even impossible—at times.

Because of this, my team has learned and grown more than most. In my career, I've been able to mentor hundreds of entry-level personnel to management, thirty-two managers to director positions, and seven manager/director-level people to executives.

That's a pretty decent track record. But it comes with a lot of sacrifice from the employee/mentee. I am brutally honest about all that.

I don't want some dramatic or sad moment four months from now because I pretended it was all rainbows and butterflies. I don't want to waste my time and energy or focus on someone who isn't here for the long haul.

4.3 Onboarding

The onboarding of new employees is vitally important. First impressions matter, but what matters more is making sure that your staff learns about your vision and how their contribution fits in.

Day one at my companies generally looks like this:

1. Onboarding paperwork—state requirements, contracts, NDAs

2. HR SOPs—review policies that have to do with HR, like holidays, etc.

3. Vision and company history—where we've been and where we are going. I used to do this one-to-one, but that is not scalable, so we now have a recording and a little quiz at the end to make sure they understand it.

4. Listen to two podcasts. These are all about the company and what we do, as a way to get them more up to speed with how the business really works.

5. Read some blog posts about how I think teams should be treated. These are hand-selected from my personal blog so readers can get to know me and my philosophy.

6. Write a one-page essay on what Shockwave does. If they don't get this right, we start again on day two, but they are not allowed to move on from here until they have an in-depth understanding of what we do.

On day two, they get passed on to their supervisor, so they can train at their actual job.

No one gets to this without understanding what I'm trying to do here.

As part of your team, this person represents your company and you. Take the time to train them on the company's culture and essence and the expectations of their behavior.

Your organization may be too large for you to meet with each new hire, and that's okay.

An easy fix is to create a video of you talking about your vision and where your company started. To make this less awkward, record your interview with your next hire and have someone edit it so it's easy to watch.

Be sure to talk about the culture you have built and why you've gone in that direction. While in-person time will never be replaced by a video, it is better that your employees hear directly from you on this subject. The people they report to can answer questions, but you should handle the overall subject matter personally.

Emma Rant:

There is NOTHING worse than telling this to a CEO or visionary entrepreneur and then having them make a mass production of it. Six months later, and with 25k in production costs, I have a two-hour video no one can follow.

Turn on your Zoom, hit record, and do a screen share on your WAVE. Walk us through it in twenty minutes or less. BOOM. Impactful.

From here, the direct supervisor takes over onboarding, but we have a full plan for each department that follows new hires closely over their first thirty days.

After thirty days, we ask them to review the onboarding process, the company, their department, and their direct supervisor. We continue this process after sixty and ninety days.

After their first ninety days with us, they move into a quarterly review, during which they are reviewed on their projects, the number of projects they completed on time, and how well they fit into the company's values. This continues each quarter that they're with us.

Once we have completed our review of them, we ask them to review their position. Do they have enough resources to complete tasks assigned to them effectively? Are there improvements we can put in place to make their time with us more enjoyable? What would need to happen to make this their dream job?

That last one is my favorite question. If the answer is money (I know I pay my people well), then I know they are not the type of driven individuals I want long-term on my team. But if they answer with things like:

- Resources to accomplish their tasks more effectively
- A course that will make them a better operator/executor
- A Virtual Assistant[6] to take some of the mundane tasks that are beneath them

Then I know they are a long-term fit, and I will always make sure their wants are taken into consideration.

4.4 Team Building

Team building is of vital importance to growing your organization.

If one team member isn't in sync with the rest of the team, it can poison the entire organization. While larger corporations may see an impact only on the department that person works in, we tend to have smaller teams in direct response/eCommerce, so one person can greatly impact the organization as a whole.

---

6   A Virtual Assistant (VA) is a remote professional who provides administrative, technical, or creative assistance to clients, typically from a home office. VAs are employed across various industries to handle tasks such as scheduling, email management, data entry, social media management, and customer support, allowing business owners to focus on core activities by delegating routine tasks.

One misaligned person slowly starts to poison everyone, day-by-day, shifting the morale of even well-laid-out company cultures. One bad apple really does spoil the bunch.

Team building means getting your team to act as a team, not as individuals rowing against each other. It's about getting them in sync and allowing every member of the team to understand where everyone else is coming from, what's driving them, and what they best respond to.

When I talk about this subject, I get a little disorganized and scattered, for the same reason I'm so good at team building—because I know how to flow with the person or group I am talking to.

I can have a full plan for what I am going to talk about, and with one sentence from the group I'm talking to, I can shift completely to content THEY need to hear instead.

Here's how my kind of team building looks in practice.

While I regularly do small things to build my team and have tons of incentives to create the culture I am looking for, I am very intent on having in-person, departmental team building at least once every other year.

I enjoy using two methods, depending on the team's level of experience.

Method One: For higher-level managers and executives who are decision-makers.

Before we meet for our in-person team building, I give them two books to read as a group: *The Five Dysfunctions of a Team*, and *Overcoming the Five Dysfunctions of a Team*. In these books, author Patrick Lencioni perfectly lays out the process of building a team that can debate and be committed to the path they decide upon.

He helps create a team that is willing to be wrong, holds each other accountable, and flows together for the best outcome for the company.

I love this process. It's phenomenal. I've tried to change it a bit to be more "my" way, but you really cannot improve this system. The teams I've worked with that put effort into reading these books together, reviewing the sections together, and doing the exercises generally shift into a well-balanced team of A-players practically overnight.

At this point, we go into the exercise that I run for people without management or leadership experience.

Method Two: For people who do not have experience in management or leadership (or step two for people who do).

I generally like to have everyone do the Myers-Briggs test from 16Personalities offsite before we begin in-person team building. The test determines people's personalities, placing them into one of sixteen personality categories. It's an incredibly useful tool for understanding, supporting, and building your team.

Once we are all together, I have each person tell the group which of the sixteen personalities describes them. If anyone shares the same personality, I group them together. Then we read aloud certain sections from each description for each of the personalities represented in the group. More on that in a second.

This really gives a deep understanding of how each person thinks, how they want to be communicated with, what is important to them, and how to approach them. Each personality is different in each of these aspects.

Emma Rant:

The worst thing we were all taught as children is that you should do unto others as you would have done to yourself, or treat others as you want to be treated.

That's a super selfish statement.

Every one of the sixteen personality types prefers to be talked to and treated differently, based on their personality. Some people like direct, honest opinions; others prefer a softer approach.

I once had a girl say she needed communications in writing because she became anxious if she had to talk to me directly about a problem or issue.

Writing it out and allowing her time to process helped her not only understand the problem but come up with a way to resolve it without anxiety. She is a brilliant creative, so learning this about her not only helped her do her job better, but it also took a lot of stress away from me, because this allowed her to fix the issues in her department without any intervention from me.

Almost every time I have a "people" problem in one of the companies I manage, it is because someone said something that pissed someone else off. It is almost ALWAYS not what they said but how they said it.

Imagine a world where we were taught how to approach people with information, both good and bad, with the intention of achieving the best possible outcome.

Here's how I start to go through those personality types:

I start with myself. I always go first, and I always show the most vulnerable side of myself. Remember, we cannot make good progress with teams if they are afraid or unwilling to be vulnerable with one another.

I am the Executive Personality (shocked, right?).

The first thing you see in this personality test is the score. Here is mine, for reference. This explains exactly where you sit in each of the categories that the test reviews. The score usually doesn't come up in team building, but it explains why two people with the same personality type aren't going to be *exactly* the same, which can often be worth explaining, particularly when team members seem confused.

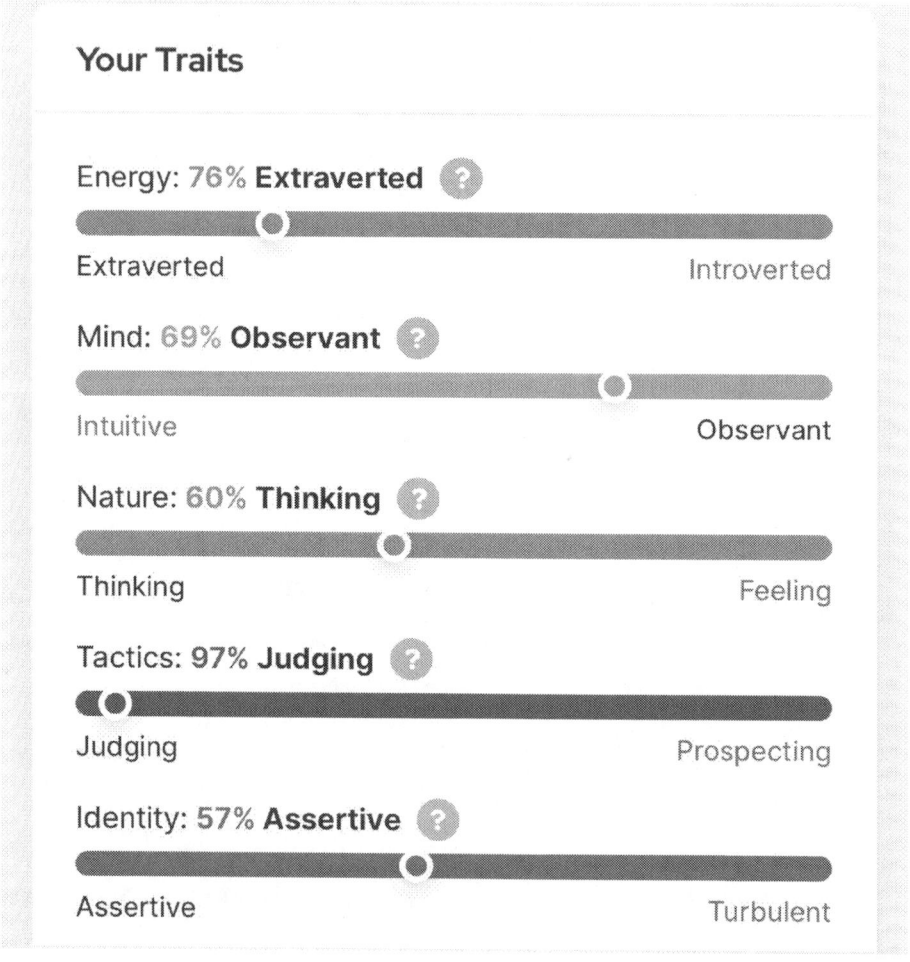

Your Traits

Energy: 76% **Extraverted**

Extraverted — Introverted

Mind: 69% **Observant**

Intuitive — Observant

Nature: 60% **Thinking**

Thinking — Feeling

Tactics: 97% **Judging**

Judging — Prospecting

Identity: 57% **Assertive**

Assertive — Turbulent

From that point, I move on and read out the introduction for my personality, giving an overview of what motivates people with my particular personality type. Below, I'm attaching an image of that introduction.

Introduction

WHO IS THE EXECUTIVE PERSONALITY TYPE?

ESTJ (Executive) is a personality type with the Extraverted, Observant, Thinking, and Judging traits. They possess great fortitude, emphatically following their own sensible judgment. They often serve as a stabilizing force among others, able to offer solid direction amid adversity.

> ## Good order is the foundation of all things.
>
> Edmund Burke

People with the ESTJ personality type (Executives) are representatives of tradition and order, utilizing their understanding of what is right, wrong, and socially acceptable to bring families and communities together. Embracing the values of honesty and dedication, ESTJs are valued for their mentorship mindset and their ability to create and follow through on plans in a diligent and efficient manner. They will happily lead the way on difficult paths, and they won't give up when things become stressful.

ESTJs are classic images of the model citizen: they help their neighbors, uphold the law, and try to make sure that everyone participates in the communities and organizations that they hold so dear.

Leading by Example

Strong believers in the rule of law and authority that must be earned, ESTJ personalities lead by example, demonstrating dedication and purposeful honesty and an utter rejection of laziness and cheating. If anyone declares hard, manual work to be an excellent way to build character, it's ESTJs.

This personality type is aware of their surroundings and lives in a world of clear, verifiable facts. Their surety of their knowledge means that, even against heavy resistance, they stick to their principles and push an unclouded vision of what is and is not acceptable. And their opinions aren't just empty talk either, as ESTJs are more than willing to dive into the most challenging projects, improving action plans and sorting details along the way, making even the most complicated tasks seem easy and approachable.

People with the ESTJ personality type are dedicated individuals who pride themselves on always finishing what they start, rendering them reliable and trustworthy.

However, ESTJs don't work alone, and they expect their reliability and work ethic to be reciprocated – people with this personality type meet their promises, and if their partner or coworkers jeopardize them through incompetence, laziness, or, worse still, dishonesty, they do not hesitate to show their disappointment. This can earn them a reputation for inflexibility, but it's not because ESTJs are arbitrarily stubborn but rather because they truly believe that these values are what make society work.

A Greater Responsibility

The main challenge for ESTJ personalities is to recognize that not everyone follows the same path or contributes in the same way. A true leader recognizes the strength of the individual as well as that of the group and helps bring those individuals' ideas to the table. That way, ESTJs really do have all the facts and are able to lead the charge in directions that work for everyone.

This immediately gives them a simple overview of my personality and who I am as a person. In a lot of cases, people see exactly how accurate this description is, which gives them a level of buy-in that normally takes time to achieve. For many people, it's easier to see how a personality type describes someone else than it is to say, "This describes *me*." Getting that clarity makes the team building move much more smoothly.

Next, I move on to Strengths and Weaknesses, reading off each section. As I read, people will say things like, yeah, I can see that, or yup! That is you! It's important to be flexible here, as this is all about building up that buy-in, making the team building as productive as possible.

ESTJ Strengths

- **Dedicated** – Seeing things to completion borders on an ethical obligation for people with the ESTJ personality type (Executives). Tasks aren't simply abandoned because they've become difficult or boring. Often refusing to cut corners or shirk responsibilities, they showcase their dedication through their unwavering commitment to high standards. In fact, they tend to strive for perfection in most things that they take on in life.

- **Strong-willed** – A strong will makes this dedication possible, and ESTJs don't give up their beliefs because of simple opposition. They defend their ideas and principles relentlessly and must be proven clearly and conclusively wrong for their stance to budge.

- **Direct and Honest** – ESTJs trust facts far more than abstract ideas or opinions. Straightforward statements and information are king, and people with this personality type return the honesty (whether it's wanted or not).

- **Loyal, Patient, and Reliable** – ESTJs work to exemplify truthfulness and reliability, considering stability and security very important. When ESTJs say they'll do something, they keep their word, making them very responsible members of their families, companies, and communities.

- **Enjoy Creating Order** – Chaos makes things unpredictable, and unpredictable things can't be trusted when they are needed most. With this in mind, ESTJs strive to create order and security in their environments by establishing rules, structures, and clear roles. They tend to exemplify this need for order in their home lives as well, as they are the most likely personality type to have a very structured schedule that includes fixed times for waking up and going to sleep.

- **Excellent Organizers** – A commitment to truth and clear standards makes ESTJs capable and confident leaders. People with this personality type have no problem distributing tasks and responsibilities to others fairly and objectively, making them excellent administrators.

ESTJ Weaknesses

- **Inflexible and Stubborn** – The problem with being so fixated on what works is that they too often dismiss what *might* work better. Everything is opinion until proven, and ESTJ personalities are reluctant to trust an opinion long enough for it to have that chance.

- **Uncomfortable with Change** – ESTJs are strong adherents to tradition. When suddenly forced to try unvetted solutions, they become uncomfortable and stressed. New ideas suggest that their methods weren't good enough, and abandoning what has always worked before in favor of something that may yet fail risks their image of reliability.

- **Judgmental** – People with the ESTJ personality type have strong convictions about what is right, wrong, and socially acceptable, and their compulsion to create order often extends to all things and everyone, ignoring the possibility that there is more than one right way to get things done. They do not hesitate to let people they disagree with know what they think, considering it their duty to set things right.

- **Too Focused on Social Status** – ESTJs take pride in the respect of their friends, colleagues, and community, and while difficult to admit, they are very concerned with public opinion. These personalities can get caught up in meeting others' expectations, failing to address their own needs.

- **Difficulty Relaxing** – This need for respect fosters a need to maintain their dignity, which can make it difficult for ESTJs to cut loose and relax for risk of dropping the ball or looking the fool, even in good fun.

- **Difficulty Expressing Emotion** – People with the ESTJ personality type get so caught up in the facts and most effective methods that they forget to think of what makes others happy – they forget to express emotions and empathy. For example, a detour can be breathtakingly beautiful and a joy for the family, but this type may only see the consequence of arriving at their destination an hour late, hurting their loved ones by rejecting the notion too harshly.

From that point, we skip through the sections on Romantic Relationships, Friendships, and Parenthood. Depending on the team, we may cover some parts from these sections later, but right now we're focusing on the team. We've opened ourselves up to be vulnerable, and we can address some of the listed personality traits and how they resonate in each of us.

When I get to the part about reliability and how I feel when my subordinates jeopardize that, I take it past the piece of paper that outlines my personality. I speak directly about the anxiety it causes me and how I won't be able to sleep or think of anything else.

When they hear that, they start to understand why I get so upset when we deliver even one day late. It's like the end of the world for me. Sharing how this makes me feel helps them see that I'm not being inflexible or stubborn; I am truly having a meltdown because my personality type just cannot handle not delivering on a promise I've made. If I know ahead of time, I can reset the expectations, and together we can all avoid an unpleasant experience.

Once I have opened up and let everyone see that side of me, it's far easier for them to do the same. That becomes particularly true after I read aloud how my personality type requires reciprocation.

This is where the magic happens.

I take each person and have them read off their introduction, and then both their strengths and weaknesses, getting everything out for open discussion.

Now, go around the room and have each person discuss how one of that person's strengths could help them improve, and what strengths they have that can assist that person with their weaknesses.

For example, as an executive personality, my strength is the ability to create order. One of my weaknesses is being uncomfortable with change.

I can help a teammate who struggles to create order or processes, and they can help me see that sometimes change is necessary to create the most effective way of completing a process.

We continue this process section-by-section until everyone has shared. Once we are done, we move on to the Career Path and Workplace Habits sections, with everyone reading their section before we move on to the next.

By the time you are done with this, your team will have a completely new perspective on one another.

It's truly amazing how this carries over. Moving forward, they know how to approach each other, and they feel more connected, so they are more willing to "contribute" to one another by calling each other out and holding each other accountable. You know you have done a great job when they hold *you* accountable on calls.

A team that has trust in each other and can be vulnerable is truly a remarkable accomplishment. Once you get everyone on the same team, all you can do is win!

4.5 Management vs. Mentorship

Given how important both are for people development, I am often asked what the difference is between management and mentorship. Let me break it down.

Management and mentorship are two essential roles in personal and professional development, and each plays a distinctive part.

4.5.1 Management

Management involves overseeing a team or organization and ensuring that tasks are accomplished efficiently, and objectives are met. Managers maintain control over processes, allocate resources, and supervise performance to maintain structure and productivity.

Managers prioritize meeting organizational goals and deadlines, often with a results-driven focus. They ensure compliance with standards and keep their team aligned with company strategies.

Managers effectively oversee daily tasks by using organizational, planning, and problem-solving skills. Their approach can often be transactional, focusing on key performance indicators and accountability.

Management relationships are often hierarchical and transactional; respect is demanded due to the authority and expectations of the role.

4.5.2 Mentorship

Mentorship is the guidance and advice given by more experienced individuals to less experienced ones, aiming to help them grow, develop skills, and achieve their career goals. It is a relational approach focused on fostering potential and personal development.

Mentors emphasize the long-term development of their mentees, providing advice that goes beyond immediate job requirements. They build trust to encourage growth, career progression, and confidence.

Mentors leverage interpersonal, listening, and coaching skills to inspire and empower mentees. They tailor their guidance to individuals' needs, strengths, and aspirations.

Mentorship relationships are based on mutual respect and trust, where mentees seek mentors' advice voluntarily. Mentors aim to inspire rather than direct their mentees.

Despite the differences in these roles, managers can also be effective mentors if they incorporate a more developmental mindset into their managerial responsibilities. This dual role allows them to guide team members while nurturing their potential.

Understanding these distinctions and integrating both roles where appropriate can lead to a more holistic approach to leadership.

I try to develop managers into mentors at my companies and the companies I manage.

The more people I can have on my team who assist in the development of staff, the faster I can scale that company. While not everyone should be left to mentor others, as many do not hold the emotional IQ, discernment, or the ability to let go of their own ego, some managers will take this opportunity and not only flourish personally, but help you expand and grow as well.

Once you have determined that someone on your team would make a great mentor, you will need to be intentional about how you mentor *them*. Even the people who make the best mentors need to learn how to best support those they teach.

Mentorship can be a lifetime commitment and should really be worth your time. Mentoring someone who is not obsessed with growth, who argues instead of learns, or whose ego gets in their own way more than it doesn't is simply a waste of your time. Be sure to focus your resources and time on the right people.

For some resources on how I mentor my mentees, please go to www.readscope.co/tools for templates like:

Connection Cadences

How to Keep Track

Setting Boundaries

Pulse Checks

Part 5 -
Execute —> Move

In Part One of this book, I discussed how to create your company's WAVE. This is the foundational framework through which your company establishes where it is going (your 1-10 Year Vision), the guiding motivation for the path it will take (Absolute Focus), the kind of person who is going to get it there (Values Driven Future), and the first part of the system you'll use to keep on track (Execution Plan).

In this section, I'll go in depth on that execution, taking you through the Operational Framework by which your company will live and breathe. One of the hardest components of a successful business isn't defining what the business is, or coming up with the products, or even deciding how to sell them. The hardest part is actually executing the plan while staying focused.

We will be reviewing:

- Quarterly Meetings/Goal Setting: In these meetings, we will review our One-Year commitments and determine what milestones we must pass to achieve those commitments by year end.

- Breakers: These are weekly or biweekly meetings to keep things on track. We will review our quarterly goals to make certain they are on track and discuss any roadblocks or bottlenecks that arise.

- Unification Meetings: These are quick monthly touchpoints between CEO and COO or Visionary and Integrator to ensure each is unified and on the same page. All relationships take work, and the relationship between these two can be as challenging as a marriage. Unification meetings keep the two in sync.

- Meetings and Communications: To keep everything moving forward, there are necessary meetings and communications that have to happen. We will create a simple cadence for these so your team can function without your involvement.

5.1 Quarterly Meetings and Goal Setting:

Quarterly Goals are the catalyst for achieving your yearly commitments. Every three months, you will evaluate your yearly commitments and determine which milestones you need to pass in order to stay on track. You will choose five to fifteen goals per quarter, depending on team size, resources, and how difficult it is to accomplish them.

Each quarter, prior to the quarter's end, you will meet with the key members of your team to review the quarter that is ending and to set the next quarter's goals. The first time you do this, it will be all about planning future quarterly goals.

During every meeting thereafter, you will need time to review the past quarter and that future planning. Make sure you discuss without blame what went well, what didn't, what could have been improved, and how to make it work next time.

Each commitment should be reviewed at length regarding where things stand and what needs to happen by the end of both the next quarter and the year. Goals will naturally come up while discussing each commitment.

You will keep a running list of these goals during the meeting. Once you have reviewed each commitment, it is time to review each proposed goal, who will be assigned that goal, and what resources are needed to accomplish the goal.

Once you have a well-detailed list, review those goals one more time with the totality of all the goals in mind, as well as each person's day-to-day responsibilities to the company. This will give you a clear indication of everyone in your team's capacity. If you've got a team member who's swamped, managing a dozen people and twenty projects, they're probably not going to be able to take on a goal requiring ten hours of their time a week.

Once capacity has been established, you can choose which goals are most important to pursue and which should be left for the next quarter or assigned to vendors. Remember, your goals are not aspirational or "nice to have"—they're a list of tasks that will be completed by the end of the quarter.

It's important to get staff buy-in here. The last component of our quarterly meeting is to ask our staff if they agree that they can commit the time necessary for completing this goal by the proposed due date.

Note: When setting deadlines, not all quarterly goals should be pushed out to the end of the quarter. You will find that if something takes two weeks and you give your staff three months, they will take all three months. Additionally, there may be a cadence of tasks that need to be completed in a certain order for the overall goal to be completed. Timelines and due dates are imperative and should be achievable and reasonable.

Now that you have staff buy-in and everyone is in agreement on the goals for this quarter, you need to keep a good eye on where things are to keep everything on track. Waiting until the next quarter to review will be disastrous. At Shockwave, we use Breakers to keep all tasks on track.

5.2 Breakers

Breakers are ninety-minute meetings where we take a step back from working *in* the business to work *on* the business. This meeting is designed to monitor your quarterly goals and any roadblocks, bottlenecks, or anything else that your core team should be aware of.

Your company will set up weekly or biweekly meetings where all key staff will follow a specific agenda. This will not be "death by meeting," where a ton of chatting and small talk go on. There is no room for that. This will be the platform by which you will keep your finger on the pulse and ensure that everything is on track and *stays* on track.

Moving forward, your business will no longer think of time from week to week, month to month, or quarter to quarter. Everything will be Breaker to Breaker. Time will be described as "by the next Breaker" or "by the first Breaker of next month I will..."

You will meet with your team at the cadence you choose. I suggest starting with weekly, and if you need less, decrease to every other week. If you find you are not achieving milestones, then you can go back to weekly. This is not one-size-fits-all, so play around a little until you get it right for your business.

Everyone is forced to come together, slow down, and assess everything with precision. It's also a roundtable of accountability, because issues are called out and brought to a resolution right then and there.

The meeting is on the same day, at the same time, each week, biweekly, or monthly to your choosing. The day and time never change. Everyone needs to be on the call and knows not to schedule anything during that time. This will seem difficult at first, but once it becomes part of your company, it will get easier and easier. No doctor's appointments, sales calls, flights, or anything else.

The only acceptable reason for someone not to be on the call is that they are on vacation or sick. That's it. Otherwise, we are on the call following the formula we put together. This will seem difficult at first, but once it becomes part of your company, it will get easier and easier.

We have had some wonderful experiences running these. Having everyone "in the know" and in full understanding of what is happening in every department is a great way to keep the needle moving.

I've certainly had visionaries throughout the years who called these meetings fluff and gave me a ton of flack over them. But once they implemented Breakers, every one of those visionaries, including my own business partner, Travis, admitted there had been a dramatic shift in their organization.

So let's get into it.

5.2.1 Meeting Agenda

1. Meeting Opening: Personal Accounts
2. KPI review
3. Quarterly Goals
4. Updates
5. Movers
6. Signals
7. Meeting adjourned on time, every time

5.2.2 Meeting Opening: Personal Accounts

Everyone QUICKLY states

- What they are grateful for
- What they are excited about
- A personal or professional win

5.2.3 KPI Review

Review all your departmental KPIs (You should not have more than ten to fifteen). You need to dive deep only if a number isn't on track. For example, if you are an online seller, one of your KPIs is likely your refund rates.

If this is at or below the goal, there is no reason to spend valuable time discussing the subject. Your department head clearly has it under control. If the refund rate is higher than the goal, then you can add that item to the Signals List for in-depth discussion.

In all likelihood, the department head added it to the list prior to the meeting. But if not, simply add it to the list and move on to the next KPI. To keep the meeting efficient, do your best not to allow a bunch of conversations to run out of place.

We keep our KPIs on a simple spreadsheet, and each person responsible for the KPI fills in the sheet the day before our Breaker is scheduled.

Emma Rant:

Far too often, I see business owners ramble on during meetings, inserting their ideas or adding context that is just not necessary to keep things on track. This meeting is to review where we are, where we plan to be, and alert each other to anything that puts that in jeopardy. Stay on the agenda and do not deviate, or you will find these meetings less and less effective.

5.2.4 Quarterly Goals

Review each person's assigned Quarterly Goal(s). Review what they have accomplished toward getting this goal completed since the last Breaker.

This is when you need to be very intentional about holding staff accountable. Before you know it, the quarter will be over, and if you allow them just to say everything is "on track," you will likely see no real movement on their goal at the end of the quarter.

You want them to post updates from Breaker to Breaker on what they did to work on this goal or what they were waiting to work on. Again, our staff fills this in on the day before our Breaker is scheduled.

We keep track of all this in ClickUp, so everything is in place. But it's totally up to you whether you want to keep it in a project management tool, on a document, or elsewhere.

Each person who has a goal must keep all updates up-to-date and all accompanying information in the goal within ClickUp. This allows us to keep a close eye on true progress.

As we review goals with our staff, we discuss next steps and what needs to be accomplished to keep the goal moving forward until the next Breaker. This is essentially a to-do list that will keep all goals moving to completion. We call these movers. We keep track of them and identify them by deliverable, placing them on our movers list.

5.2.5 Movers

Once we have reviewed everyone's goals, we quickly review the movers list from the previous Breaker. Each mover should be completed before the Breaker, so there should not be much to review. If there are leftover movers, particularly those that have not been discussed up to this point, this indicates a roadblock or lack of progress.

5.2.6 Signals List

Signals are roadblocks, bottlenecks, problems, or even pending disasters that we need the whole team to be aware of. We call them Signals because I do not like to shine a negative light on anything, even if it seems justified. Everything is an opportunity to learn, achieve, and grow, and presenting these as emergencies or problems creates a negative atmosphere that limits effectiveness.

I am signaling everyone to this thing that we all need to be aware of and mitigate, if possible. My team's most productive discussions come from the Signals component of the Breaker. This time allows us to brainstorm and for everyone on the team to contribute.

During the preparation at the end of the day before the Breaker, staff will go in and add Signals to the list. Throughout the meeting, as things come up, we add to the Signals. In the end, we usually have a list of things to cover, which we quickly put in order of priority.

Most of the items are discussed on the call, but remember, we end the meeting on time every time. Therefore, some Signals may be held off until the next Breaker, and some are assigned for a few members to discuss after the meeting. Since we talk about the highest-priority Signals first, this is not generally an issue; but if there is a signal that needs more time and attention, schedule a brainstorming meeting with as many key staff members as necessary. The point is to keep things moving and advancing.

5.2.7 Meeting Adjourned on Time, Every Time

That is your Breaker. If you adopt this meeting for one quarter, stick with it, and don't try to change it in the first quarter, you will see massive improvements in your business.

5.3 Unification Meetings

As discussed at the beginning of this book, unification meetings are an essential part of the Visionary/Integrator relationship. These relationships can be extremely rewarding and empowering, or miserable and a constant struggle. The meetings determine which kind of relationship you will have.

It is important that the visionary and integrator function as a unit, on the same page and completely unified.

The number of times you meet each quarter depends on your business and what is going on. Are you in maintenance mode? Building mode? Scaling? All of these require different meeting cadences.

At Shockwave, we've dealt with clients who own several businesses, some of which were brand new launches, with others bringing in seven to nine figures. There are a lot of moving parts all the time, so we needed frequent meetings. We've also had clients that were doing 100 million but only sold a few products in one niche.

I met each quarter with one of these clients for our unification meeting, and I barely heard from her in between. As she had a WAVE, I knew what she wanted executed, so there wasn't much to discuss. You will need to determine how much change and movement are likely in your business and then plan accordingly.

Always book more than what you need. You can always claim back your time.

You can always have a unification call if there is a concern about getting off track. A set time will be more productive, but there is nothing wrong with saying, "We're getting off track," or "I'm not sure we are unified. Can we hop on a call?"

Overall, I think having a monthly or quarterly unification meeting that is on the books makes the most sense. The Visionary/

Integrator duo should start with a monthly schedule and see if it makes sense to move it to quarterly.

Emma Rant:

I have a client who changes his mind way too often if I leave him sitting too long. We meet twice weekly. I have to make sure we are in full alignment each Monday and again on Thursday, or he will derail the whole company.

Another client I had was very much capable of letting go. She recognized that she is the best person in the world to run the vision for the company and that I am the best person to run operations. We met once per month for fifteen to twenty minutes. That is all we needed. We got on the same page and moved on with the actual work.

Needless to say, I could accomplish far more for her as a COO than for the guy I meet with twice weekly. She and I maintained a good Visionary/Integrator relationship, and therefore, the company reflected that.

That is not to say the client who needs calls multiple times a week is wrong. He just needs to be handled differently. Obviously, I was able to accomplish a lot more for her than I can for him, but at the end of the day, each Visionary/ Integrator duo is different, and it's essential to give the visionary the time they need to get on board. As long as they allow their integrator to execute, it's right.

I have a previous client whom I met daily—yes, freaking DAILY—for the first year. That turned into twice a week. It took a long time to get him there, but we eventually moved to once a month. It's all about the visionary's comfort and trust level, as well as the integrator helping them learn their role.

If they have made it work monetarily while throwing wrenches at their staff, it will be really hard to unlearn those behaviors. That is perfectly okay—every visionary works in a different way.

If the visionary needs to have a brainstorming session, so be it. If the integrator is starting to get resentful or frustrated by the behavior of the visionary, it is time for a unification meeting.

Note: Visionaries NEED brainstorming sessions. They have a million ideas a day, and they need someone to talk them through everything. This can feel like a waste of time for an integrator, particularly for a busy one, but it is imperative to make time for them.

Out of every 100 ideas they have, there is likely one nugget of PURE GOLD that can increase the company's bottom line. Visionaries need the integrator to help them pull that one idea out of the 100 and execute it at the right time.

I have been so fortunate to serve as an integrator to quite a few visionaries over the years. It has really been my life's joy.

While I discuss how much work the Visionary/Integrator relationship can be, I want to make sure I highlight how rewarding it can be when you are unified and working together. Having the same mindset, values, and opinions and unity plays an integral role in how rewarding or how frustrating the relationship will be.

I've had some phenomenal experiences with visionaries in my career. I was the COO and Integrator of one visionary's company for three years. She and I have spent a lot of time understanding each other.

We vibed in a way I had not experienced before. We were able to just roll with things because we understood each other's *why* intimately.

We once had a business meeting where we were trying to acquire a company. Without any planning or thought, the three-hour meeting was seamless. Throughout the meeting, we knew what the other was thinking and kept setting up the conversation so the other could knock the answers out of the park.

Looking back, we probably could not have planned that meeting to go better.

It was all the time we spent together understanding each other's wants and whys. We knew each other well enough that all that it took was a look across the table to know exactly what the other was trying to communicate.

That was a *fire* experience for me. The true value of the unification meetings had never been clearer than at that moment. While most of our understanding of one another came from annual and quarterly meetings, those once-a-month unification meetings helped us stay in continued alignment. I could go a month without talking to her directly and still be completely connected to her vision. It shows on each monthly alignment call.

Another one of my previous visionaries had built an empire pretty much by himself. What he has created blows my mind.

Our working relationship was a little rocky at the beginning. We aligned in the basic structures of how we thought about the world, but we had not spent nearly enough time talking about those things. But once we started to meet regularly, one-on-one (which was hard to get him to do), we became surprisingly close and very much aligned.

Fast forward half a year and we were consulting each other on almost everything. We could talk effortlessly and endlessly about anything and everything. Our relationship had grown, and we ended up having an intense trust in one another. We put in the time, and it was so worth it.

The last example I have is a seemingly negative one. I had a visionary who felt she was too important to get on the unification calls. We had them booked once a month, but no matter how I tried to include her, she just refused. She felt it was a waste of her time if we weren't talking about a specific product or problem.

Unfortunately, after several months of working with her, we were so out of alignment that everyone was miserable. My staff, her staff, and every vendor that worked on that project was unhappy. Travis finally stepped in, and for the sake of Shockwave's employees, he fired them as a client while I was attending a mastermind[7]. I was so grateful. I was at a total loss as an integrator on how to integrate.

There is a big part of me that felt as though I had failed, but in the end, not every visionary is for every integrator. If you're not aligned, it's just not going to work. You've got to put in the work to make it pay off.

It's important to mention that if the visionary and integrator are not aligned in the way they think about overall values, they will *never* be aligned on how to run the business. It just won't work.

That is okay. It happens.

Move on quickly for the sake of everyone. It's not about one person being a better visionary or one being a better integrator. That isn't a thing. It's all about alignment.

I am arguably one of the best integrators in direct response. I'm not trying to be conceited, but you likely will not find many integrators who can match me.

I do not say that to toot my own horn. I'm a true integrator, so I am comfortable in the shadows and do not need any kind of recognition. I'm saying that to really drive home the fact that if you

---

7 A Mastermind group is a peer-to-peer mentoring concept where individuals with similar interests, goals, or challenges come together to share knowledge, support each other, and solve problems collectively. These groups typically consist of business owners, entrepreneurs, or professionals who meet regularly to exchange ideas, provide feedback, and hold each other accountable for achieving their goals. The collaborative nature of a mastermind helps participants leverage the collective intelligence and experiences of the group to advance their personal or professional development.

are not a match by personality, then no matter how good you are at your job, it just won't work, any more than a marriage between two people who are not aligned in morals and values.

5.4 Meetings and Communication

Staff always need to have one-off meetings and to stay in regular communication. You don't want to micromanage this communication, but if your company doesn't have a communications policy, your staff will likely talk across many channels, causing confusion and disorganization.

There should be a direct policy of where to communicate what.

For example, if you are discussing a project, task, or goal, everything should be communicated within the project management tool that the task lives in, so that it is all in one place.

Slack is fine for random questions or updates, but your team needs to understand that communications can be a distraction that will degrade the quality of work. We have set times throughout the day for responding to Slack messages, emails, and questions or directives in the project management tool, and that should all be scheduled between concentrated work blocks.

Having this set communications strategy will keep everyone on track and in a concentrated work state. Organization is key to efficiency, and when people are chatting randomly all over the place, they wind up wasting time looking for things and trying to find communications that could be anywhere.

I also encourage you to encourage your staff to hold one-off quick meetings to discuss projects or roadblocks. Too often, particularly in remote online teams, we try to resolve issues or questions with text messages. This takes far longer than a two-to-three-minute conversation, as there is just so much context lost in texting.

With all of this in place, you've set up your team for success. You've established a clear cadence of meetings that take you closer to your goals, rather than wasting everyone's time. You've got a system for internal communications that ensures that everyone has a space to ask the questions they need to ask—and to have those questions answered. Your team is ready to execute.

Part 6 - Conclusion

As I wrap up *SCOPE: A Direct Response/eCommerce Marketer's Guide to Business*, I want to reflect on the journey we've taken through this book and bring out some of the most relevant points from each part.

I've written SCOPE to give entrepreneurs and business leaders direct access to what I've learned in my career and to summarize the lessons from dozens of masterminds and boardroom meetings, hundreds of business books, and countless hours of work with visionaries.

Setting Your Vision taught us the importance of a clearly articulated and compelling vision, and how you present that vision to your team. We learned that vision is not just a statement; it's a strategic foundation that aligns and motivates your team toward common goals. I've shown you the WAVE method, giving you a structure to take your vision from an idea into actionable strategies by creating your Written Vision, Absolute Focus, Values-Driven Future, and Execution Plan.

Creating Processes showed the necessity of creating stream-lined, efficient processes, how to build those processes, and how creating those processes improves your operational performance. By systematizing and documenting routine tasks, we don't just ensure consistency and reliability for those tasks, we improve our outcomes. We've also talked through how documenting these processes allows for continual improvement as we refine and develop each task.

Operational Excellence was all about upgrading operations and transforming functional operational coasting into real excellence, efficiency, and effectiveness. Operations is about constantly driv-ing your profit margin as you scale, and keeping ahead through strategic planning, resource management, and continual im-provement. Operational Excellence means staying ahead in the competitive landscape of eCommerce.

People Development focuses on a business's core asset—its people. Investing in the development of your team is not just ben-eficial, but essential for the long-term sustainability of your busi-ness. We explored how fostering a culture of continuous learning, leadership, and mentorship creates a competent and motivated workforce aligned with the company's objectives, and we talked through some of the systems I use to build and align teams.

In Execute -> Move, we talked through the process of turning plans into action and the systems we use to create realistic but meaningful goals, get buy-in from your team on these goals, and keep those goals on track through the year. This final pillar of the SCOPE framework ties it all together, ensuring that the vision you've set, the processes you've built, the operations you've implemented, and the people you've trained execute with excel-lence, changing your vision from a dream into a tangible reality.

Remember, the journey to excellence is ongoing. eCommerce is constantly evolving, and your approaches need to evolve along with it. SCOPE is not about setting a static, non-evolving system in place. It's about giving you the operational tools to navigate as the world develops, so you can lead your business to continual new heights.

"SCOPE" is more than just a guide; it's a strategic partner that supports your journey toward eCommerce excellence. As you turn the final page of this book, I hope you've gained some new perspective on your operations, and that you're ready to turn your vision into a clear, concrete plan that everyone on your team deeply understands and buys into.

If you are interested in any of our services, you can learn more by visiting our websites:

Shockwave Solutions - Operations:

www.shockwavesolutionsllc.com

Seismic Wave Support - Customer Service:

www.seismicwavesupport.com

AfterShock Consulting - 1:1 COO Coaching:

www.aftershockmentoring.com

SurgeMail - Email List Management: www.surgemail.co

About the Author

Emma Rainville is the Co-Founder of Shockwave Solutions, LLC. An accomplished operations specialist, Emma specializes in working with visionary entrepreneurs in the Direct Response and eCommerce spaces, turning their visions into a profitable, scalable, and sustainable reality.

Having scaled businesses to 9-figures in annual revenue; turned directionless companies into clear, aligned enterprises; and spoken on some of the industry's biggest stages, Emma has solved countless operational issues. Now, she's ready to share her system so you can do the same.

Made in the USA
Columbia, SC
07 February 2025

52720382R00102